Kenya

a Lonely Planet travel atlas

Kenya – travel atlas

1st edition

Published by
Lonely Planet Publications
Head Office: PO Box 617, Hawthorn, Vic 3122, Australia
Branches: 155 Filbert St, Suite 251, Oakland, CA 94607, USA
                   10 Barley Mow Passage, Chiswick, London W4 4PH, UK
                   71 bis rue du Cardinal Lemoine, 75005 Paris, France

Cartography
Steinhart Katzir Publishers Ltd
Fax: 972-3-699-7562
email: 100264.721@compuserve.com

Printed by
Colorcraft Ltd, Hong Kong
Printed in China

Photographs
Dawn Delaney, David Else, Hugh Finlay, Roger Jones and David Wall

Front Cover: Batik of market scene (Hugh Finlay)
Back Cover: Mount Kilimanjaro is a stunning backdrop for the Amboseli National Park wildlife (David Else)
Title Page: Young Samburu woman (David Else)
Contents Page: Makonde carvings (Hugh Finlay)

First Published
April 1997

Although the authors and publisher have tried to make the information as accurate as possible, they accept no responsibility for any loss, injury or inconvenience sustained by any person using this book.

National Library of Australia Cataloguing in Publication Data

Finlay, Hugh.
    Kenya

    1st ed.
    Includes index.
    ISBN 0 86442 442 6.

    1. Kenya - Maps, Tourist. 2. Kenya - Road maps.
    I. Finlay, Hugh. (Series : Lonely Planet travel atlas).

912.676

Contents

Hugh Finlay

After deciding there must be more to life than civil engineering, Hugh took off around Australia in the mid-70s, working at everything from spray painting to diamond prospecting, before hitting the overland trail. He joined Lonely Planet in 1985 and has written *Jordan & Syria*, co-authored *Morocco, Algeria & Tunisia* and *Nepal* and has contributed to other LP guides including *Africa, India* and *Australia*. He lives in central Victoria, Australia, with his partner Linda and their daughters Ella and Vera.

About this Atlas

This book is another addition to the Lonely Planet travel atlas series. Designed to tie in with the equivalent Lonely Planet guidebook, we hope the *Kenya travel atlas* helps travellers enjoy their trip even more. As well as detailed, accurate maps, this atlas contains a multi-lingual map legend, useful travel information in five languages and a comprehensive index to ensure easy location-finding.

The maps were checked on the road by Hugh Finlay as part of his preparation for a new edition of Lonely Planet's *Kenya* guide.

From the Publishers

Thanks to Danny Schapiro, chief cartographer at Steinhart Katzir Publishers, who researched and drew the maps with the assistance of Michal Pait-Benny and Iris Sardes; Iris also prepared the index. At Lonely Planet, the maps and index were checked and edited by Lou Byrnes. Louise Keppie-Klep was responsible for all cartographic checking, design, layout and cover design. The back cover map was drawn by Paul Clifton and the illustration was drawn by Kathy O'Loughlin.

Lou Byrnes coordinated the translations. Thanks to translators Yoshiharu Abe, Christa Bouga-Hochstöger, Adrienne Costanzo, Pedro Diaz, Megan Fraser, Elisabeth Kern and Nick Tapp.

Request

This atlas is designed to be clear, comprehensive and reliable. We hope you'll find it a worthy addition to your Lonely Planet travel library. Even if you don't, please let us know! We'd appreciate any suggestions you may have to make this product even better. Please complete and send us the feedback page at the back of this atlas to let us know exactly what you think.

Sudan

Ethiopia

Somalia

Uganda

Rift Valley

Eastern

North Eastern

Lake Turkana

Lokichokio

Lokitaung

Kakuma

Lodwar

Kalokol

North Island
North Island National Park

Sibiloi National Park

Central Island
Central Island National Park

Lokichar

North Horr

Loyangalani

South Island National Park

South Horr

Marsabit
Marsabit National Reserve

Moyale

Banissa

Takaba

Buna

Mandera

Wajir

Mado Gashi

Losai National Reserve

Laisamis

Parsaloi

Baragoi

Maralal

Wamba

Maralal National Sanctuary

Shaba National Reserve

Buffalo Springs

Samburu National Reserve

South Turkana National Reserve

Nasolot National Park

Ngirang

Loruk

Laikipia National Reserve

Kabernet

Kerio Valley / Kamnarok National Reserve

Kapenguria

Kitale

Saiwa Swamp National Park

Webuye

Mount Elgon National Park

Bungoma

Busia

Malaba

Eldoret

Maralal Mari National Park

B9

D504

D500

C81

A2

C77

B4

A1

C46

C113

B4

C51

A1

C45

C42

A104

C81

C83

B9

B9

D57a

C79

C78

B9

MAP LEGEND

Number of Inhabitants:

NAIROBI		500,000 - 1,000,000
MOMBASA	◉	250,000 - 500,000
MACHAKOS	◎	100,000 - 250,000
Thika	◉	50,000 - 100,000
Muranga	◎	25,000 - 50,000
Kilifi	◉	10,000 - 25,000
Gumba	○	<10,000

NAIROBI
Capital City
Capitale
Hauptstadt
Capital
首都

✪ Capital City (Locator map)
Capitale (Carte de situation)
Hauptstadt (Orientierungskarte)
Capital (Mapa Localizador)
首都（地図上の位置）

NAKURU
Provincial Capital
Capitale de Province
Landeshauptstadt
Capital de Provincia
地方の中心地

International Boundary
Limites Internationales
Staatsgrenze
Frontera Internacional
国境

Provincial Boundary
Limites de la Province
Landesgrenze
Frontera de Provincia
地方の境界

Major Highway
Route Nationale
Femstraße
Carretera Principal
主要な国道

Highway
Route Principale
Landstraße
Carretera
国道

Regional Road
Route Régionale
Regionale Fernstraße
Carretera Regional
地方道

Secondary Road
Route Secondaire
Nebenstraße
Carretera Secundaria
二級道路

Unsealed Road
Route non bitumée/piste
Unbefestigte Straße
Carretera sin Asfaltar
未舗装の道

Railway
Voie de chemin de fer
Eisenbahn
Ferrocarril
鉄道

Route Number
Numérotation Routière
Routenummer
Ruta Número
道路の番号

99
Distance in Kilometres
Distance en Kilomètres
Entfernung in Kilometern
Distancia en Kilómetros
距離（km）

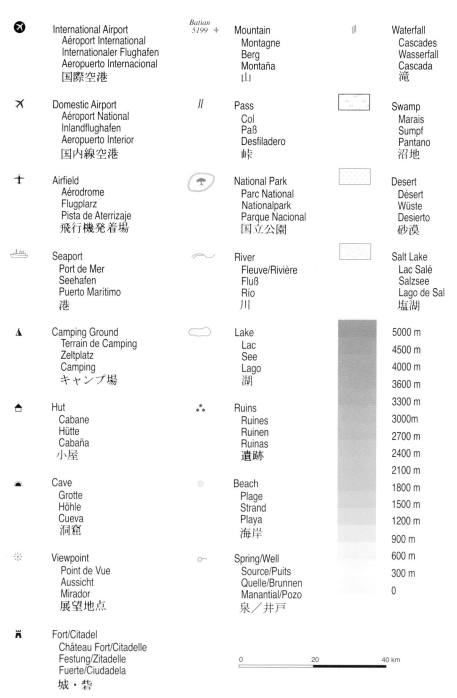

✈ (circle)	International Airport Aéroport International Internationaler Flughafen Aeropuerto Internacional 国際空港	*Batian* *5199* +	Mountain Montagne Berg Montaña 山	Waterfall Cascades Wasserfall Cascada 滝
✈	Domestic Airport Aéroport National Inlandflughafen Aeropuerto Interior 国内線空港	∬	Pass Col Paß Desfiladero 峠	Swamp Marais Sumpf Pantano 沼地
✝	Airfield Aérodrome Flugplarz Pista de Aterrizaje 飛行機発着場		National Park Parc National Nationalpark Parque Nacional 国立公園	Desert Désert Wüste Desierto 砂漠
	Seaport Port de Mer Seehafen Puerto Marítimo 港	～	River Fleuve/Rivière Fluß Río 川	Salt Lake Lac Salé Salzsee Lago de Sal 塩湖
▲	Camping Ground Terrain de Camping Zeltplatz Camping キャンプ場		Lake Lac See Lago 湖	5000 m 4500 m 4000 m 3600 m
⬠	Hut Cabane Hütte Cabaña 小屋	∴	Ruins Ruines Ruinen Ruinas 遺跡	3300 m 3000m 2700 m 2400 m 2100 m
◗	Cave Grotte Höhle Cueva 洞窟	◌	Beach Plage Strand Playa 海岸	1800 m 1500 m 1200 m 900 m
※	Viewpoint Point de Vue Aussicht Mirador 展望地点	⌒	Spring/Well Source/Puits Quelle/Brunnen Manantial/Pozo 泉／井戸	600 m 300 m 0
♜	Fort/Citadel Château Fort/Citadelle Festung/Zitadelle Fuerte/Ciudadela 城・砦			

0   20   40 km

Projection: Universal Transverse Mercator

1 : 1 000 000

A B C D

1

2

3

4

5

6

34°E

5°N

35°E

Nangolet

Kapoeta

S u d a n

Loyuro River

Lolimi

Lomeyen River

Tarach River

SUDAN

KENYA

A1

Mogila
1698

Lotikipi Plain

Lotagipi Swamp

Kialon

Lauru

Mogila Range

39

Lokichokio

Nanam River

Rift Valley

Nare

Larema

Lotuke
+ 2797

2148

Sogot Mountain

Natira River

Napas River

Tarach River

Pelekech Range

4°N

Kidepo Valley
National Park

KENYA
UGANDA

Pirre

Morungole
+ 2749

Kamion Oropoi

104

Kakuma

Muruu Ngithigerr (Loima Hills)

Lomej

Apoka
Rest
Camp

Apoka

Morungole

Kalabi

Katarum
Lodge

Magos

Lwala
+ 2456

Napararo

U g a n d a

Sogwass
2086 +

Karenga

Kaabong

Lobuneyt

Mugei
2040

Risai

Katorosa
+ 2040

▼16▼

Depeth River

1916

69

Tarach River

E   F   G   H

1

2

3

4

5

6

36°E

Ethiopia

Kaiemothia
Lukulan

Kathiren
+ 1701

Lorionetom Range

Nawakaiya
+ 1767

Liwan

Kelam

Omo River

Lobuni

Lokinach

Dande

Macho Afas River

Gingere   + 820

1246
+

Kokuro

Kaikworr

Kakelaiw

Kokilis

Namuruputh

Lapurr Range

Lapurr
+ 1481

Todenyang

ETHIOPIA

KENYA

Ft. Banya

46

Lomoru Itae

Lokitaung

Iléret

854
+

▼12▼

Kubi Fara

Karori

+ 559

Crocodile
Sanctuary

North Island

Murua Rith Hills

Siboloi
National Park

Eastern

Murangering

Lake Turkana

Derati

104

Koobi Fora

Allia Bay

Derati

31

Kalimapus Hills

Kalokol River

Ferguson's Gulf

Kalekol   6

▼17▼

Central Island
Central Island
National Park

Gajos

Gajos

B4

Kotome River

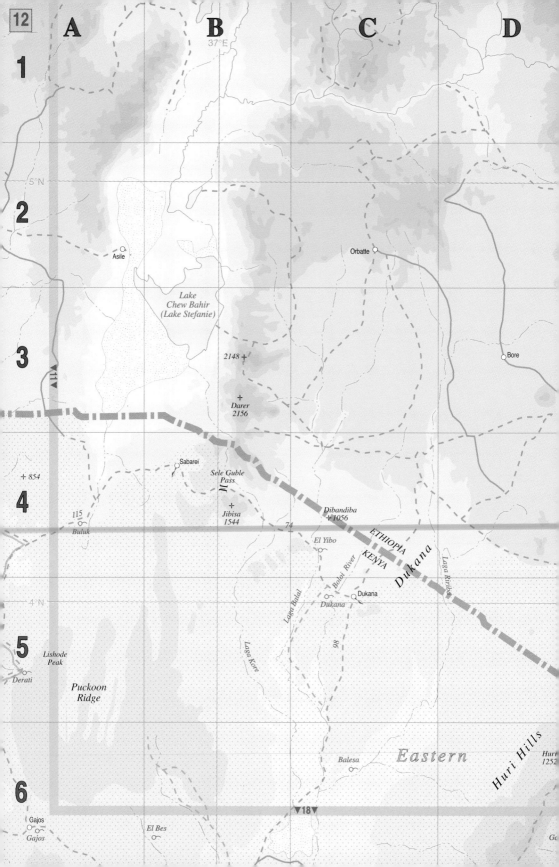

12

A   B   37°E   C   D

1

5°N

2

Asile

Orbatte

Lake Chew Bahir (Lake Stefanie)

Bore

3

2148 +

▼11▼

Darer
2156 +

+ 854

Sabarei

Sele Guble Pass

4

115
Buluk

Jibisa
1544 +

74

Dibandiba
+ 1056

El Yibo

ETHIOPIA

Dukana

Laga Biribo

KENYA

Boloi River

Dukana
Dukana

Laga Batal

4°N

5

Lishode
Peak

Derati

Laga Kore

98

*Puckoon
Ridge*

Eastern

Huri Hills

Balesa

Huri
1252

6

Gajos

Gajos

El Bes

▼18▼

Go

E F G H

1

2

3

4

5

6

38°E

39°E

Yabelo

Hudat

Digalu

Arero

159

Fudalhi River 44

Chumba

Camo

101

Web

Wachile

Sidamo

100

G. Ess
1637

Ethiopia

Faille

1525

Gamud
+ 2579

Adilli

105

Mega

112

Mega Escarpment

El Leh

25

Forole
2008

Ngaso Plain

ETHIOPIA

KENYA

Agal Guda
1500 +

Moiale

Kwial
+ 1159

Sololo

▼19▼

Laga Walde

Ariya

A2

Moyale

Shinil Plain

▲14▲

14

A   B   C   D

1

40°E

2

5°N

○ Hudat

Guba ○

3

Dawa Parma

Blanga ○

Dawa Wenz

Budde ○

El Medera ○

Mittita ○

Sidamo

4

Dembeldoro ○

Chelago ○

5

○ Adilli

ETHIOPIA

Korille ○

5°N

KENYA

El Roba ○

Juldessa
+ *1836*

Banissa ○

D504

121

El Der ○   *El Der*

123

○ El Leh

85

Laga Sure

79

El Warsesa ○

6

▼13▼

▼20▼

Malab
+ *1403*   Gurar ○

Dandu
1262 +

Takaba ○

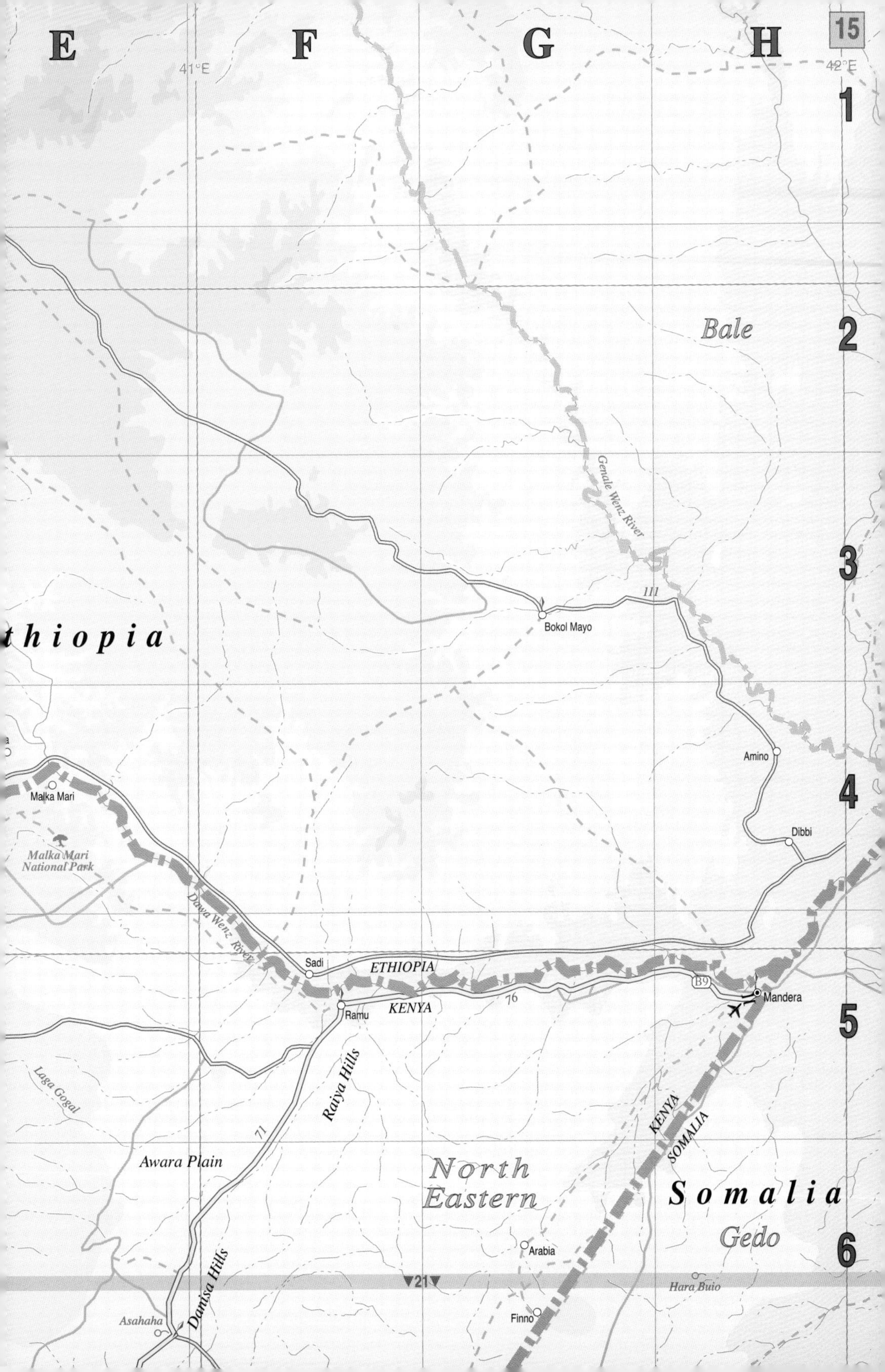
E
F
G
H
41°E
42°E
1
2
3
4
5
6
Bale
Genale Wenz River
111
Bokol Mayo
thiopia
Amino
Malka Mari
Malka Mari National Park
Dibbi
Dawa Wenz River
Sadi
ETHIOPIA
KENYA
Ramu
76
B9
Mandera
Laga Gogal
Raiya Hills
71
KENYA
SOMALIA
Awara Plain
North Eastern
Somalia
Gedo
Arabia
▼21▼
Hara Buio
Dantsa Hills
Asahaha
Finno

A   B   C   D

1

2

3

4

5

6

34°E

69

+1916

29

▲10▲

35°E

Koputh

Loyoro

Lolelia

Chakolomun
+
1803

Kacheri

+ 2286

Murua Ngithigerr (Loima Hills)

3°N

Murua Ngithigerr
+ 1437

Puch Prasir
Plateau

Mungyen

40

Dopeth River

Longiro River

Kotido

Nariwo

+ 1849

Panyangara

Magosi

64

Matheniko
Game Reserve

51

Ngolalaolon River

Natele River

Alerek

Kagododoga

U g a n d a

Sinyu

Lokiriama

49

KENYA

Kachom

Bokora Corridor
Game Reserve

Lokichar

Apule River

Nakiloro

UGANDA

Loiya

Morulem

Lopei

21

Mount Moroto
+ 3084

74

Lokopo

Logwelei

34

11

Moroto

Turutoko

31

Kangola

Nadunget

Nasigiriya

Okok River

Okere River

Kokeris

26

40

Katikekile

Lokitanyala

Kachago
+ 2787

16

Lotome

Lorengedwat

Kapelebyong

Lokiporangatome

68

Narithal

Loro

Karasuk Hills

Apidochot

Lorengechora

Karamoja

33

Tenus
2548

Amaseniko

Amuda

Kotaruk River

Achwa

Aketa

Adachal

Alekilek

Lothaa

Napak
+2539

Achorichor

Kanyangareng River

Kosike

51

102

Kokusa

Usuku

Kamalinga Hills

Nabilatuk

54

Amudat

2°N

Old Nariam

Ukutat River

Lalachat

34

Komolo

19

Katakwi

Nariam

24

31

Moruita

Kapel
209

Wera

31

Eastern

Pian Upe
Game Reserve

Ayass
2633 +

Namalu

Kany

Toroma

Magoro

41

+ Kadam
(Debasien Mountain)
3068

Morua

Okokorio

Peta

Muchimaket River

Kaplu

Lake Bisina
(Salisbury)

Mukara

Lake Opela

Kide

Nyero
Rock Paintings

21

Atuitui

20

Kelim River ▼22▼

Chepsikunya

Karita

Kumi

Kopenek

Ngenge

Gongelai

71

Suam River

Kabarwa

Ngoyo

E   F   G   H

1
2
3
4
5
6

Kalakol River

B4

▲11▲

36°E

Central Island
National Park

Central Island

Eastern

Eliye Springs

15

Turkwel River

Lake Turkana

Lodwar

41

51

...e River

76

Eliye Point

Lorukumu

...pirichich River

Turkwel River

Napedet Hills

Lokichar River

Kerio River

Nachorugwai Desert

Nanat
South Island

81

A1

Kakalet

+1175

Lochereesokon Hills

Loichangamatak

Kamutile Hills

Katigithigiria Hills

+
986

Kalabata

South Island National Park

Lolimo

84

Kalerut River

Loichangamatak
Hills

Rift Valley

Kalabata River

Kerio River

▼18▼

Von Höhnel Bay

Loiapuya

Lamuesseyuk

...ru

Lokichar

Loperot

Loriu Plateau

Teleki's Volcano
1194
+

Andrew's
Volcano
1067 +

C46

Lake Logipi

Auwerwer Hills

64

Kaputir

Gakong

100

57

Kangetet

Lokori

Elboiteng

Anglogitat

Nasolot National Reserve

Lebatin Plains

Kailongol
2066 +

South Turkana National Reserve

Suguta Valley

Korpu

Chepterr

Turkwel River

Nasolot

Amurwa

Wei Wei River

Lotongot

A1

Kollosia

Amaler

101

Napeitom

Suguta River

Samburu Hills

+
Sigogowa
3325

Kerio River

41

▼23▼

C113

Ruma

Akeriemet

Sigor

1369
+

Marich Pass

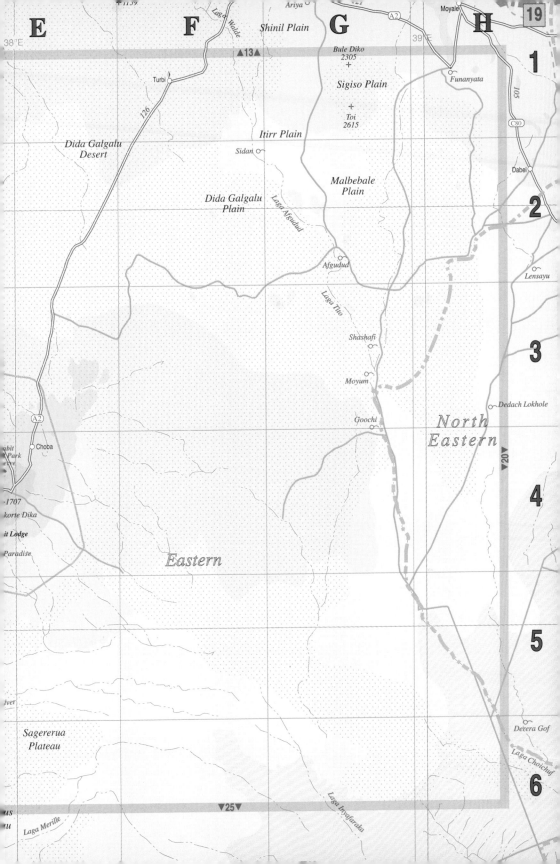

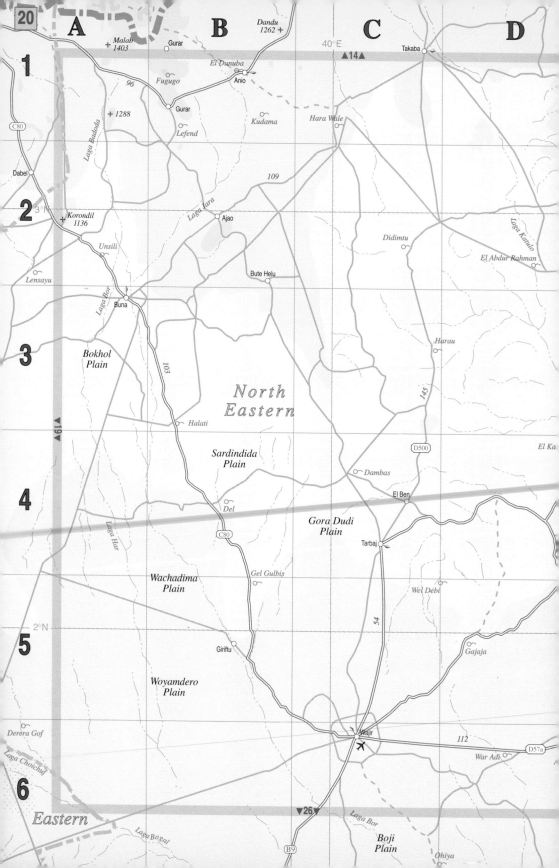

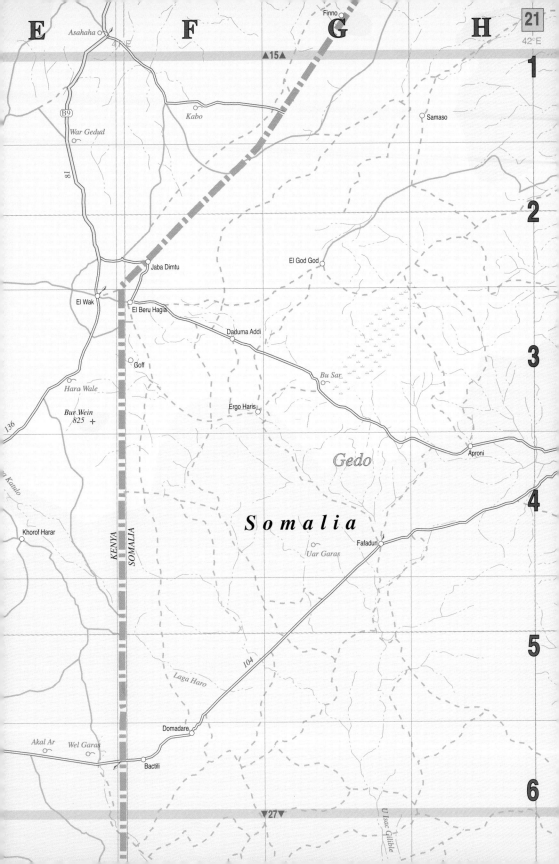

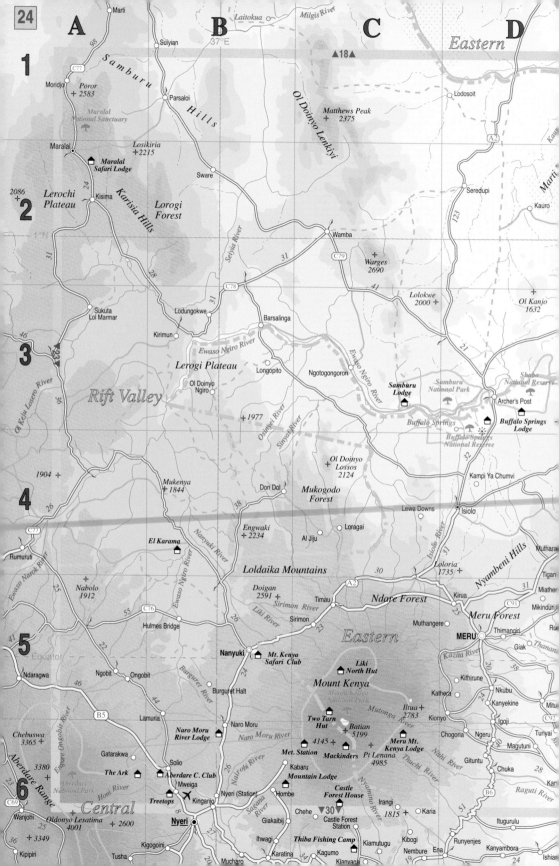

24

A | B | 37°E | C | D | Eastern

1

Marti
Suiyian
Laitokua
Milgis River
▲18▲
Lodosoit

Moridjo
C77
Poror
+2583
Parsaloi
Ol Doinyo Lenkiyi
Matthews Peak
+ 2375
A2

Samburu Hills
Seredupi
Kauro

Maralal National Sanctuary

2

2086
+
Lerochi Plateau
Maralal
Maralal Safari Lodge
Losikiria
+2215
Sware
Lorogi Forest
Wamba
C79
Warges
2690
123
Kauro

Kisima
Karisia Hills
31
28
Setiya River
31
C78
31
Lolokwe
2000 +
41
Ol Kanjo
1632

3

46
Sukuta Lol Marmar
Lodungokwe
Barsalinga
Ewaso Ngiro River
Longopito
Ngotogongoron
Samburu Lodge
Samburu National Park
Shaba National Reserve

36
Kirimun
Lerogi Plateau
Ol Doinyo Ngiro
Ewaso Ngiro River
Archer's Post
Buffalo Springs
Buffalo Springs Lodge

Rift Valley
+1977
Osinyai River
Sinyai River
Buffalo Springs National Reserve

4

1904 +
26
Mukenya
+1844
Don Dol
Ol Doinyo Lossos
2124
Mukogodo Forest
32
Kampi Ya Chumvi

C77
Rumuruti
Nanyuki River
Engwaki
+2234
Al Jiju
Loragai
Lewa Downs
Isiolo

Ol Keju Losero River
Ewaso Narok River
El Karama
Loldaika Mountains
30
Loloria
1735 +
Nyambeni Hills
Muthara
Tigan

5

Nabolo
1912
25
C76
Hulmes Bridge
Doigan
2591 +
Sirimon River
Timau
A2
Ndare Forest
Kirua
C91
Miather
Mikinduri
Meru Forest

Equator
22
55
Liki River
26
Sirimon
23
Eastern
Muthangere
25
MERU
Thimangiri
Giak
Thanano

Ndaragwa
Ngobit
Ongobit
Burguret River
Nanyuki
Mt. Kenya Safari Club
Liki North Hut
Mount Kenya
Kazita River
Nkubu
Kanyekine

46
Burguret Halt
24
Naro Moru
Mount Kenya National Park
Iltua +
2783
Kathera
Kithirune
Kionyo
Igoji
C92

6

B5
Chebuswa
3365 +
44
Lamuria
Naro Moru River Lodge
Two Tarn Hut
Batian
5199
Pt Lenana
4985
Meru Mt. Kenya Lodge
Chogoria
Ngeru
Tunyai
Magutuni

3380 +
Gatarakwa
Solio
+4145
Mackinders
Nithi River
Gituntu
Chuka
28

Aberdare Range
The Ark
Aberdare C. Club
Mweiga
Kabaru
Met. Station
Mountain Lodge
Nyumo River
Thuchi River
Raguti River

C69
Wanjohi
Oldonyo Lesatima
4001
+2600
Treetops
Kinganjo
Nyeri (Station)
Hombe
Castle Forest House
Irangi
1815 +
Karia
B6

Central
Nyeri
Giakaibij
Chehe
▼30▼
Castle Forest Station
Kiamutugu
Kibogi
Nembure
Ena
Runyenjes
Kanyambora

+3349
Kipipiri
Tusha
Kigogoini
Mucharo
Ihwagi
Karatina
Thiba Fishing Camp
Kagumo
Kianyaga
Nembure
Ishiara

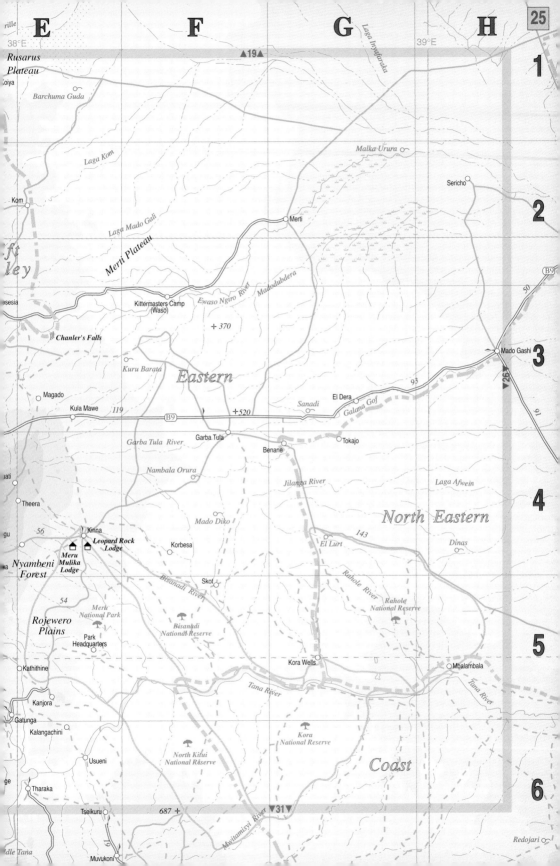

E   F   G   H

38°E   39°E

1

Rusarus Plateau

▲19▲

Lasa Insufuraka

oiya

Barchuma Guda

Malka Urura

Sericho

Laga Kom

Kom

2

Laga Mado Gali

Merti

Merti Plateau

B9

osesia

Kittermasters Camp (Waso)

Ewaso Ngiro River

Madodubdera

50

Chanler's Falls

+ 370

Mado Gashi

3

Kuru Barata

Eastern

93

▼26▲

Magado

El Dera

Galana Gof

91

Kula Mawe   119

B9

+ 520

Sanadi

Tokajo

Garba Tula

4

Garba Tula River

Benane

Nambala Orura

Jilanga River

Laga Afwein

uati

North Eastern

Theera

Mado Diko

143

gu   56

Kinna

Korbesa

El Lurt

Dinas

Leopard Rock Lodge

Meru Mulika Lodge

Rahole River

Nyambeni Forest

Skot

Rahole National Reserve

5

54

Bisanadi River

Meru National Park

Rojewero Plains

Bisanadi National Reserve

Park Headquarters

Kora Wells

Mbalambala

Kathithine

Tana River

Tana River

Kanjora

Gatunga

Kalangachini

Kora National Reserve

Usueni

North Kitui National Reserve

Coast

6

Tharaka

687 +

▼31▼

Tseikuru

Mwitamisyi River

Redojari

dle Tana

Muvukoni

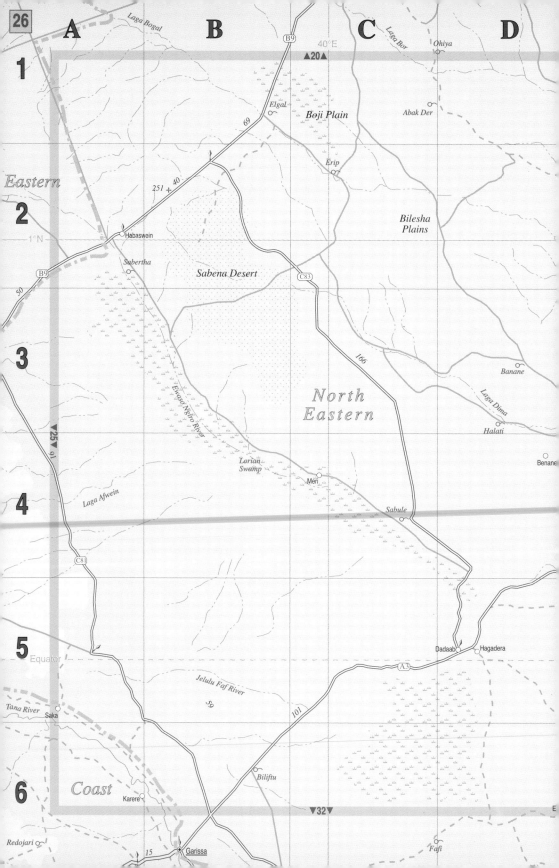

A   B   C   D

1
2
3
4
5
6

Laga Bogal

B9   40°E
▲20▲

Elgal   *Boji Plain*   Ohiya
Abak Der
Laga Bor

69
Erip

Eastern

251 × 40

1°N   Habaswein   *Bilesha Plains*

B9
.50   Subertha
Sabena Desert   C83

166   *Banane*
Laga Dima
North Eastern   *Halati*

▼25▼
91   Benane

Lorian Swamp
Méri

Laga Afwein   Sabule

C81

Dadaab   Hagadera

Equator   A3
Tana River   Saka

Jelulu Faf River
59   101

Coast   Biliftu

Karere
▼32▼

Redojari   Garissa   *Fafi*
15

Ewaso Ngiro River

1

2

3

4

5

6

Ghedu
▲21▲

Isac Gилible

Uar Garas

Uar Gallo

Lach Bissigh

Lagh Bissigh

Dif

Uar Dalado

Dudap

Meschetti

Giallo

aga Sanamai
gh

un
ains

Golgia

Bilesha
Plains

Laga Dera

KENYA

SOMALIA

Hadidca

Dobli

S o m a l i a

+128

Libol

96

A 3

Wardeglo

Hauina

Beleso Cogani

129

Rama Guda

Solola

Benuera

Caha

Rama Guda

Laga Gor anlega

Ramate

▼33▼

Wel Jara

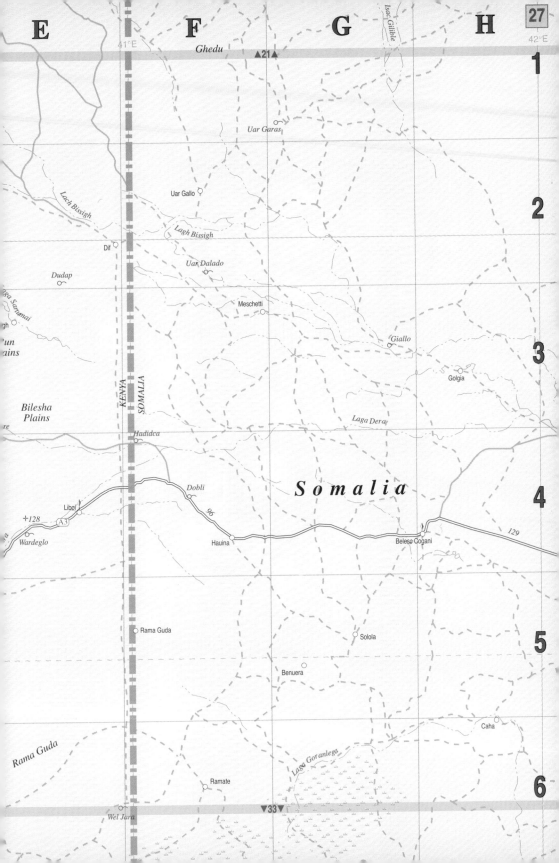

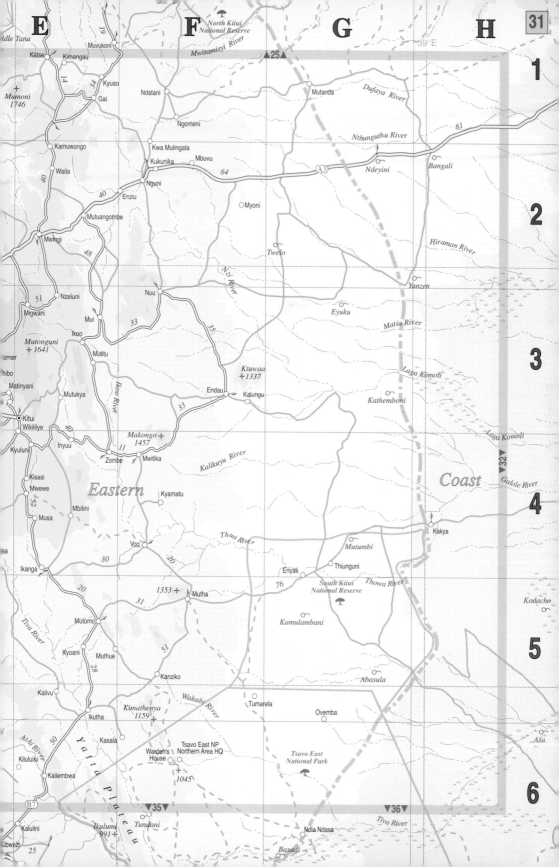

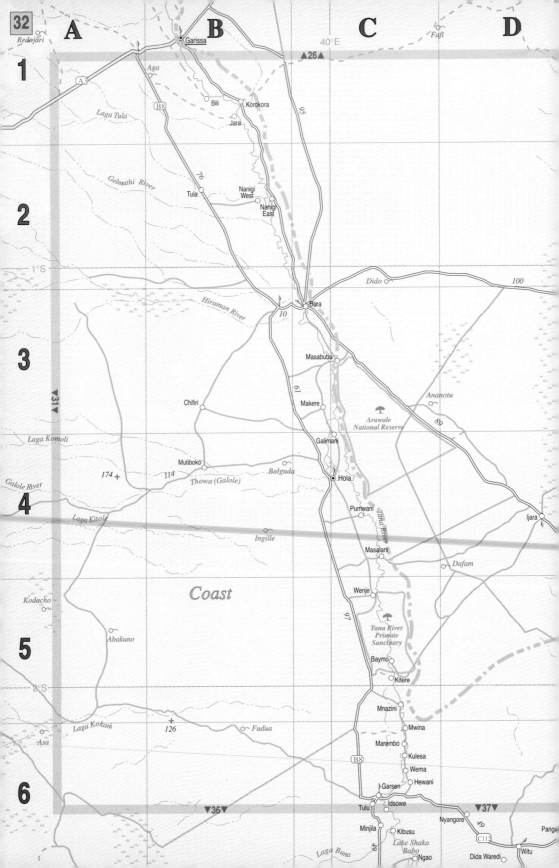

E Rama Guda **F** ▲27▲ **G** **H** 42°E

1

Giara El

Meida

SOMALIA

KENYA

Somalia

Kasha

Obe Laga Genameca

2

Bora

Ilkabere Dola

Awal Kolkole Bad Adda

Cudaio

Giu

51 Galma Galla

Kolbio

Lac Gifta Bura Buscbusc Burgavo

+ 87

Uaiore

Madero

3

Laga Garabey

North Eastern

Dodori River

Bio Gudud

Boni National Reserve

Chiamboni

Ras Chiamboni

4

Arosen River

Mararani 18 Dar Es Salaam (Shakani)

Milimani Mangai Kiunga

Kiungamwina Island

Dodori National Reserve Mambore

Kiwayu Safari Lodge 36 Simambaya Island

Kiduruni Rubu Kiunga National Marine Reserve

Majengo Oseni Ashuwei Simambaya

Kiangwe Mkokoni

Anish Kiwayu Island

Magumba Dondo Ndau Island

41 Faza Kiwayu Bay

Bargoni Magogoni Kizingitini

Paté Island Siyu

Mtangawanda Shanga Ruins

Kisingati Island

Hindi Paté Paté Bay

24 10 Mwana Manda Manda Toto Island

Mokowe Mariyamu Manda Bay

Hidio Lamu

Matondoni Shela Takwa Ruins ▼37▼

Mkunumbi Takwa Milinga

Luziwa Lamu Island Manda Island

ayatta Ras Kitau Ras Kitau

Kiongwe Lamu Bay

Msuakini Ras Tenewe

5

Indian Ocean

Mongoni Creek

Siyu Channel

River

6

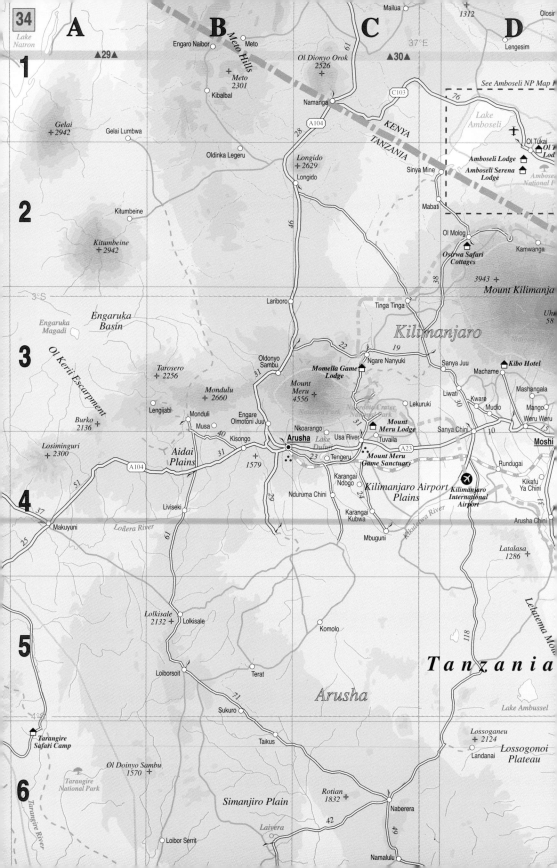

34

A   B   C   D

Lake Natron

1

Mailua
1312
Olosir

▲29▲

Engaro Naibor
Meto
Meto Hills

Ol Dionyo Orok
2526
+

▲30▲

37°E

Lengesim

See Amboseli NP Map

76

Meto
2301
Kibalbal

Namanga

C103

Lake Amboseli

2

Gelai
+*2942*
Gelai Lumbwa

A104

28

KENYA

TANZANIA

Ol Tukai
Ol
Lod

Amboseli Lodge
Amboseli Serena Lodge

Oldinka Legeru

Longido
+*2629*

Sinya Mine

Amboseli
National F

Kitumbeine

Longido

46

Mabati

Ol Molog

Kamwanga

Kitumbeine
+*2942*

Ostrwa Safari Cottages

38

3943 +

Mount Kilimanja

3°S

Lariboro

Tinga Tinga

Uhu
58

Engaruka Magadi

Engaruka Basin

Kilimanjaro

3

Ol Kerii Escarpment

Tarosero
+*2256*

Oldonyo Sambu

22

19

Ngare Nanyuki

Sanya Juu

Machame

Kibo Hotel

Mashangala

31

Momella Game Lodge

Mondulu
+*2660*

Mount Meru
4556

Liwati

Mudio

Mango

Burko
2136 +

Lengijabi

Monduli

Musa

Engare Olmotoni Juu

Nkoarango

Lekuruki

Mount Meru Lodge

31

Kware

30

Weru Weru

Losiminguri
+*2300*

40

Kisongo

Arusha

Lake Duluti

Usa River

23

Tengeru

Tuvaila

Sanya Chini

10

Moshi

Mount Meru Game Sanctuary

A23

Rundugai

4

A104

51

+
1579

Karangai Ndogo

Kilimanjaro Airport Plains

Kikafu Ya Chini

37

Liviseki

29

Nduruma Chini

24

Kilimanjaro International Airport

Arusha Chini

25

Makuyuni

Lonera River

61

Karangai Kubwa

Mbuguni

Kikuletwa River

Latalasa
1286

5

Lolkisale
2132 +
Lolkisale

Komolo

118

T a n z a n i a

Loiborsoit

Terat

Arusha

Lake Ambussel

71

Sukuro

Taikus

Lossoganeu
+*2124*

Lossogonoi Plateau

6

Tarangire Safari Camp

Ol Doinyo Sambu
1570 +

Landanai

Tarangire National Park

Simanjiro Plain

Rotian
1832 +

Letatema Mou

Tarangire River

Loibor Serrit

Laivera

42

Naberera

49

Namalulu

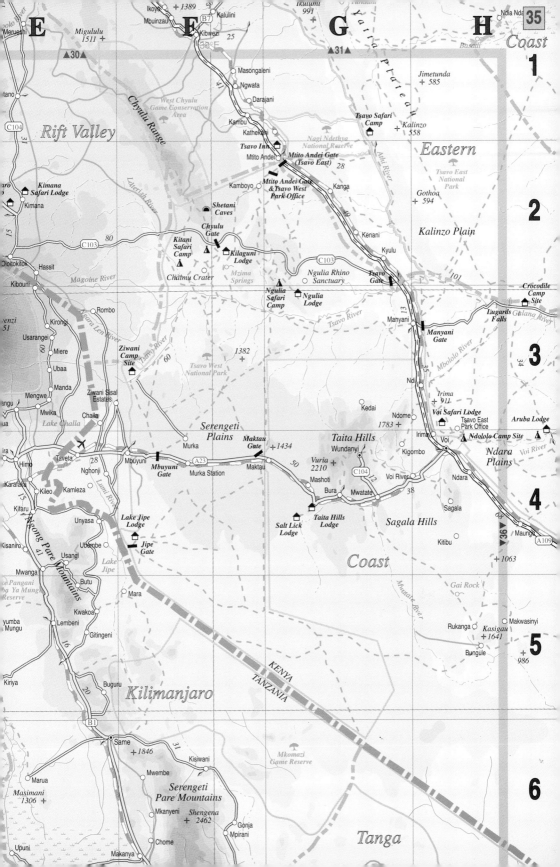

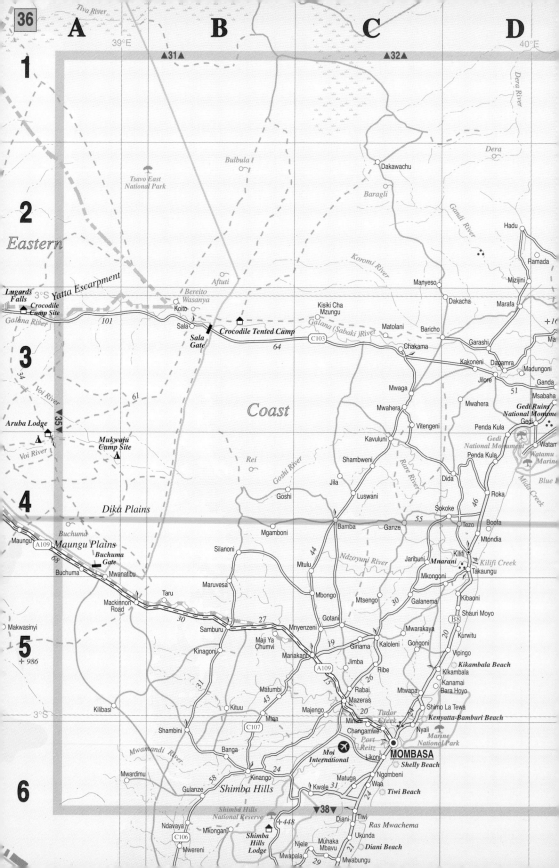

A   B   C   D

1

2

▲31▲   **▲32▲**

39°E   40°E

Tiva River

Dera River

Dakawachu

Bulbula

Tsavo East National Park

Baragli

Dera

Hadu

Eastern

Koromi River

Ramada

Manyeso   Mizijini

Gandi River

Dakacha   Marafa

3°S   *Yatta Escarpment*   *Bereito Wasanya*   Dakacha   Marafa

Lugards Falls   Koito   Kisiki Cha Mzungu   Baricho   Garashi   +10

Crocodile Camp Site   Sala   Matolani   Kakoneni   Dagamra   Madungoni

Galana River   101   Galana (Sabaki) River   Chakama   Jilore   Ganda

Sala Gate   Crocodile Tented Camp   C103   51

34   64   Mwaga   Mwahera   Msabaha

3   61   *Coast*   Mwahera   Penda Kula   **Gedi Ruins National Monument**

Gedi

Aruba Lodge   ▼35▼   Kavuluni   *Gedi National Monument*   Watam

Voi River   *Mukwaju Camp Site*   Shambweni   Penda Kula   *Watamu Marine*

Rei   Jila   Dida   *Blue*

Goshi River   Goshi   Luswani   Roka   *Mida Creek*

4   *Dika Plains*   Sokoke   46   Boofa

55   Bamba   Ganze   Tezo   Mtondia

Buchuma   Mgamboni   *Ndzoyuni River*   Jaribuni   Kilifi   *Kilifi Creek*

Maungu   *Maungu Plains*   Silanoni   44   Mkongoni   *Mnarani*   Takaungu

A109   Mtulu   Mtsengo   Galanema   Kibaoni

68   **Buchuma Gate**   Mbongo   30   B8   Shauri Moyo

Buchuma   Mwanatibu   Maruvesa   Gotani   Mwarakaya   20   Kurwitu

Taru   30   Mnyenzeni   19   Giriama   Kaloleni   Gongoni   Vipingo

Makwasinyi   Samburu   27   Maji Ya Chumvi   Jimba   Ribe   **Kikambala Beach**

5   +986   Kinagoni   Mariakani   26   Kikambala

31   A109   Rabai   Kanamai

Kilibasi   Kituu   43   Matumbi   Majengo   Changamwe   Bara Hoyo

Shambini   15   Mazeras   20   Shimo La Tewa

C107   Mtwapa   **Kenyatta-Bamburi Beach**

3°S   Mlaa   Miritini   *Tudor Creek*   Nyali   *Marine National Park*

Banga   *Mwamandi River*   24   *Port Reitz*   **MOMBASA**

Mwardimu   **Moi International**   Likoni   **Shelly Beach**

Gulanze   58   Kinango   Ngombeni

6   Mwereni   Ndavaya   *Shimba Hills*   Kwale   31   Matuga   Waa   **Tiwi Beach**

C106   Mkongani   **Shimba Hills National Reserve**   ▼38▼   Diani   *Ras Mwachema*

+448   Njele   Múhaka   Ukunda   **Diani Beach**

Shimba Hills Lodge   Mwapala   Mbavu   21

Mwabungu   29

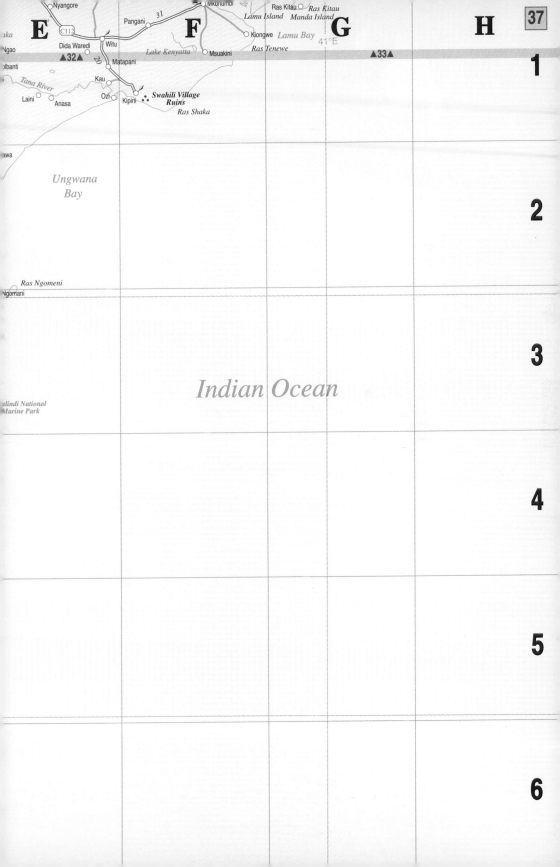

Nyangore

E C112 Pangani 31 **F** Ras Kitau Ras Kitau **G** **H**

Mkunumbi
Lamu Island Manda Island

Dida Waredi Witu Kiongwe Lamu Bay 41°E

▲32▲ Matapani Msuakini Ras Tenewe ▲33▲ **1**

20

Tana River Kau

Laini Anasa Ozi Kipini

Swahili Village
Ruins

Ras Shaka

Ungwana
Bay **2**

Ras Ngomeni

Ngomani **3**

Indian Ocean

alindi National
Marine Park

4

5

6

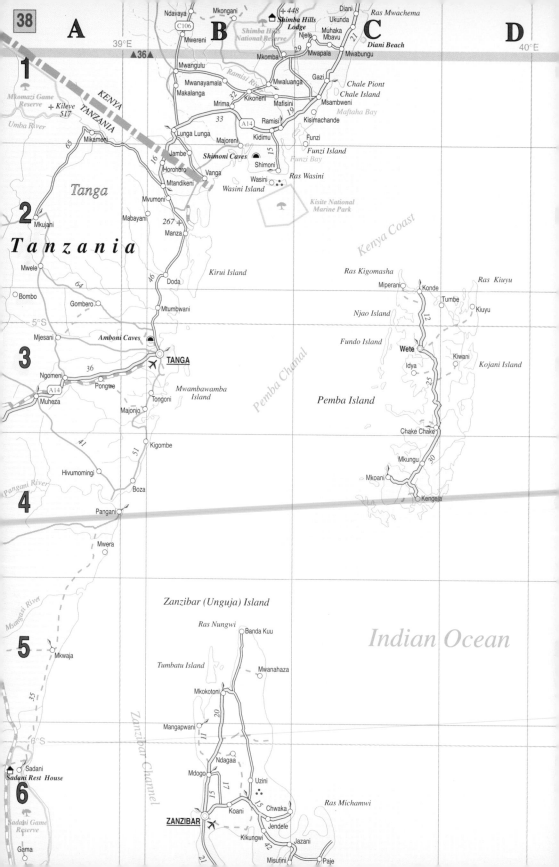

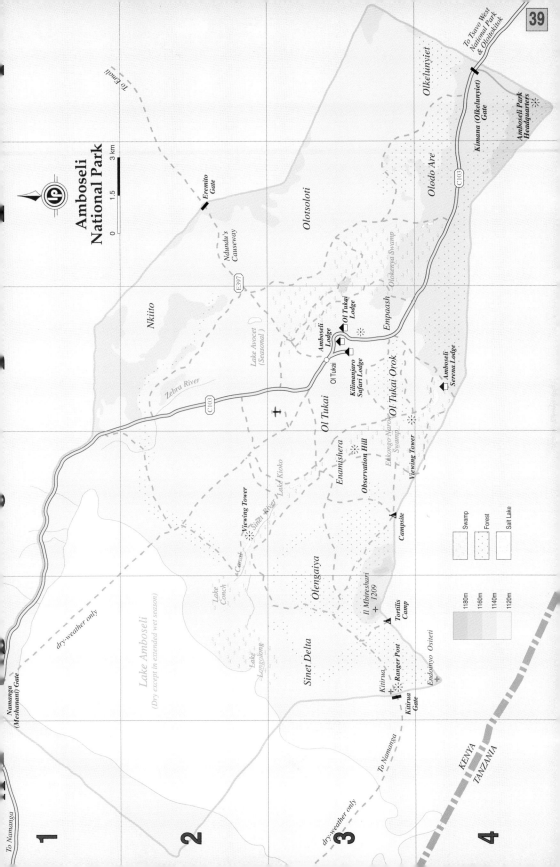

Amboseli National Park

0   1.5   3 km

Olkelunyiet

To Tsavo West
National Park
& Olotokitok

Kimana (Olkelunyiet)
Gate

Amboseli Park
Headquarters

Olodo Are

C103

Olotsoloti

Otokenya Swamp

Empaash

Ol Tukai
Lodge

Amboseli
Lodge

Ol Tukai

Kilimanjaro
Safari Lodge

Amboseli
Serena Lodge

Ol Tukai Orok

Ekkongo-Narok
Swamp

Viewing Tower

Nkiito

Eremito
Gate

Ndundu's
Causeway

E397

Lake Avocet
(Seasonal)

Zebra River

C103

Enamishera

Observation Hill

Viewing Tower

Canal

Silet River   Lake Kioko

Lake
Conch

Olengaiya

Campsite

Swamp

Forest

Salt Lake

1180m
1160m
1140m
1120m

Il Mbireshari
+ 1209

Tortilis
Camp

Lake Amboseli
(Dry except in extended wet season)

dry-weather only

Lake
Longolong

Sinet Delta

Kitirua

Ranger Post

Kitirua
Gate

Endoinyo Ositeti

To Namanga

dry-weather only

KENYA

TANZANIA

Namanga
(Meshanani) Gate

To Namanga

To Emedi

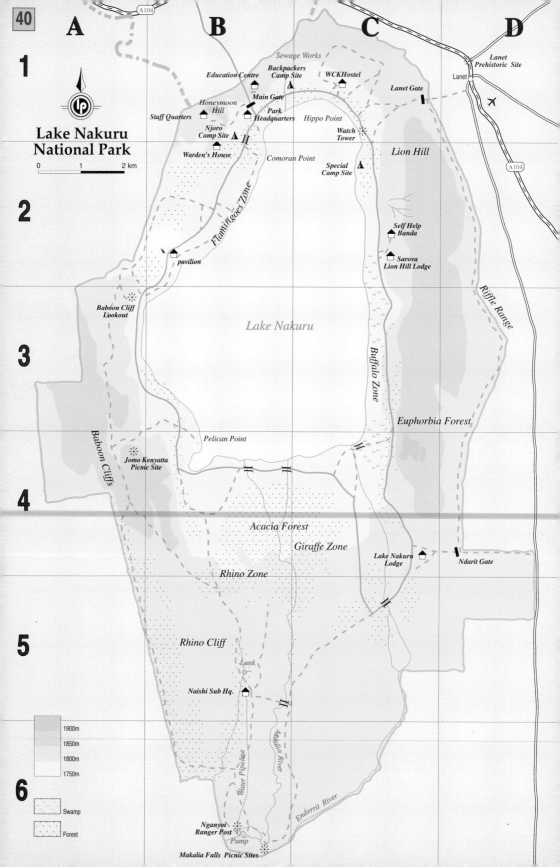

A   **B**   **C**   **D**

A104

1

Lake Nakuru National Park

Sewage Works

Lanet Prehistoric Site

Education Centre

Backpackers Camp Site

WCKHostel

Lanet

Honeymoon Hill

Main Gate

Lanet Gate

Staff Quarters

Park Headquarters

Hippo Point

Njoro Camp Site

Watch Tower

Warden's House

Comoran Point

Lion Hill

A104

2

Special Camp Site

Flamingoes Zone

Self Help Banda

Sarova Lion Hill Lodge

pavilion

Riffle Range

Baboon Cliff Lookout

Lake Nakuru

3

Buffalo Zone

Euphorbia Forest

Pelican Point

Baboon Cliffs

Jomo Kenyatta Picnic Site

4

Acacia Forest

Giraffe Zone

Rhino Zone

Lake Nakuru Lodge

Ndarit Gate

Rhino Cliff

5

Naishi Sub Hq.

Lank

Makalia River

0   1   2 km

1900m
1850m
1800m
1750m

6

Water Pipeline

Enderrit River

Swamp

Forest

Nganyoi Ranger Post

Pump

Makalia Falls Picnic Sites

Masai Mara
Game Reserve

41

Scale: 0 — 5 — 10 km

Siana Plains

Laleta

Ol Merroi River

Megwarra

Leganishu +2204

Oloolaimutia Gate

+ Mara Sopa Lodge

D301

Oloolokonya 2060 +

Ngama Hills

Masai Mara National Reserve Headquarters

Sekenani Gate

Mara Sarova Camp

Mara Wildlife Research Station

Otopilokonya

Olototikoishi

Loisekin 2080 +

Otonkai +1860

Siana Springs

Ol Losogon River

Talek River

Keekorok

C12

Longouet +1825 +

Warden's Headquarters

Keekorok Lodge

Lohukai River

Oloirtorsoit

Ol Doinyo +

Ol Ngabet Hill

Oserusopia

Oborboronyi River

KENYA

TANZANIA

Endoinyo Oloip 1690 +

Camp Site K.T.1(S)

Official Camp Sites

Camp Site K.T.2(S)

Fig Tree Camp

Talek Gate

Burrungat Plain

Posee Plains

Meta Plains

Ol Keju Gem River

Narok River

E177

E176

Kebololet Hill (Roan Hill)

Sand River

Sand River Gate

Ol Doinyo + Ol Ngabet Hill +1720

Camp Site K0.1

Camp Site K0.2

Camp Site K0.3

Emarti +1654

Ongata Olduroroi

Ol Lolduruki

Naiwashi

Mara Intrepids Club

Ongata Posee

Angarani River

Olmisigiyoi

Loldopai River

Olchorro River

Kebololet

Sand River

Serengeti National Park

Musiara Gate

Olorukoti Plain

Rhino Ridge

Mara Serena Lodge

E148

Hippo Pool

Ol Doinyo Lolaimutiak

Rhino Ridge Kiboko Crossing (Wildebeest)

Loldopai Hill +1580

Burrungat

Loldopai Hippo Pools

Sekera River

Lossirwe

Ngorbop River

Olare Orok River

Mashuru Ridge

Hippo Pool

Little Governor's Camp

Governor's Camp

Paradise Plain

Two Hills

Mara (Enkipai) River

Ol Keju Ronkai

Nolmaiman

New Mara Bridge

E176

Sirita Plateau

Oloolo Gate

Enkiti

Sanguriai

Kerinkani

Kerigedwa

Ongata Barikoi

Enikiri

Ngiro Are (Anti Poaching Unit)

Esoit Oloololo (Sirta) Escarpment

Otpurkel

Eluai Plain

Kurao Plain

The Mara Triangle

Limutu 1626

Enkoikuaatet (Salt Lick)

Noomtenterani

Crocodile Point

Mara (Enkipai) River

Road subject to flooding

Serengeti Plains

Ol Doinyo Orok

Longoroso

Epurkel Keti

Pariakelat

C13

Ol Doinyo Orok

Altitude key:
2200m
2100m
2000m
1900m
1800m
1700m
1600m
1500m

Swamp

Forest

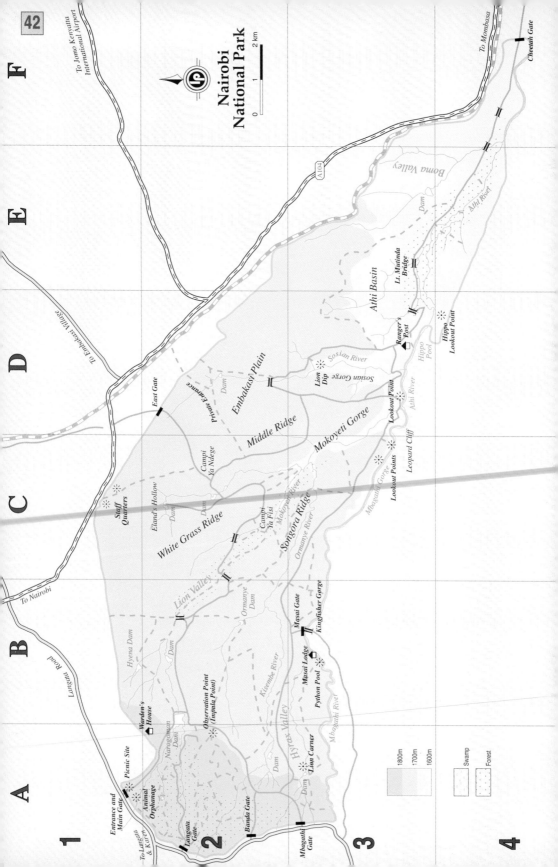

Nairobi National Park

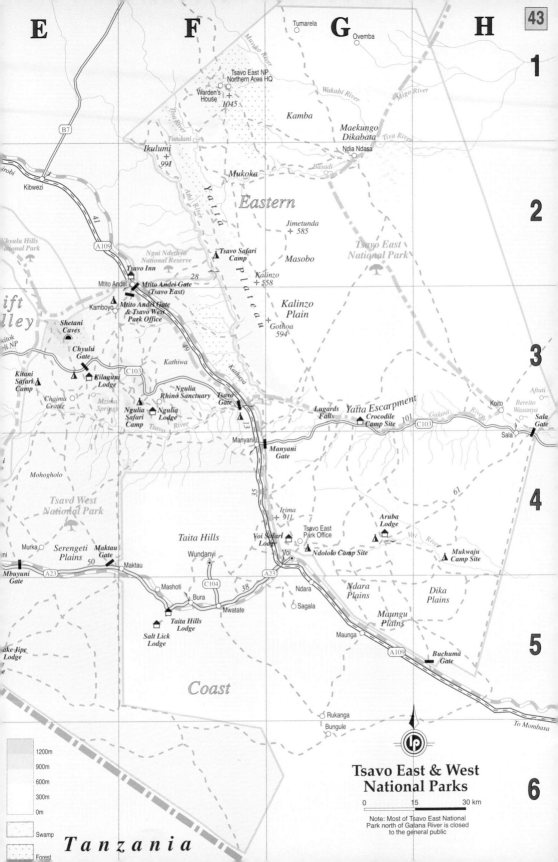

Getting Around Kenya

Bus

Kenya has a network of regular buses, matatus (normally minibuses), share-taxis and normal private taxis. The cheapest form of transport is bus, followed by matatu, share-taxi (Peugeot services) and lastly private taxi (expensive). There's not a great deal of difference in journey times between normal buses and matatus, but there's a huge difference in safety.

All but one of the bus companies are privately owned but some of them run better buses than others. Akamba Bus Service has the most comprehensive network, and has a pretty good safety record. The government bus line, KBS Stagecoach, runs modern buses, including some double-deckers, to the main towns and is also reliable and safe. Of the other private companies, Coastline, Goldline and Malindi Bus are also OK.

Some Kenyan towns have what you might call a 'bus station', although this is often nothing more than a dirt patch. In others each bus company will have its own terminus though these are often close to each other. Matatu and share-taxi ranks sometimes use the same stations as buses but this isn't always the case.

There are also a number of private 'shuttle buses' which connect Nairobi with Mombasa and with Arusha and Moshi in Tanzania. They're more comfortable than ordinary buses since they only take around 18 passengers but they are at least two to three times more expensive than ordinary buses.

Matatu

The way most local people travel is by matatu, meaning 'three' (when matatus first started running it cost three coins to travel). These can be anything from small, dilapidated Peugeot 504 pick-ups with a cab on the back, to shiny, brightly painted 20-seat minibuses complete with mega-decibel stereos, as found in Nairobi. The majority of those which do the long-distance runs, however, are white Nissan minibuses. Most matatu drivers are under a lot of pressure from their employers to maximise profits so they tend to drive recklessly and overload their vehicles. They also put in long working days. Stories about matatu smashes in which many people are killed or injured can be found daily in the newspapers. Of course, many travellers use them and, in some cases, there is no alternative, but if there is (such as a bus or train) then take that in preference. The Mombasa to Nairobi road is notorious for smashes.

As in most East African countries, you can always find a matatu which is going to the next town or further afield so long as it's not too late in the day. Simply ask around among the drivers at the bus park. Matatus leave when full and the fares are fixed. It's unlikely you will be asked for more money than the local passengers.

Train

Kenyan trains are a very popular form of travel, despite the fact that the rolling stock, tracks and other essential works have been allowed to deteriorate. The

Lioness resting in the shade

HUGH FINLAY

trains generally run on time and are considerably safer than travelling by bus or matatu. The main railway line runs from Mombasa on the coast to Malaba on the Kenya-Uganda border via Voi, Nairobi, Nakuru and Eldoret, with branch lines from Nakuru to Kisumu, Nairobi to Nanyuki, Gilgil to Nyahururu, Voi to Taveta and Eldoret to Kitale.

There are also international services between Nairobi and Kampala (Uganda) via Malaba and between Voi and Moshi (Tanzania) via Taveta. On both runs there is one train a week in either direction.

Kenyan trains have three classes of seating. First class consists of two-berth compartments with a washbasin, drinking water, a wardrobe and a drinks service. There's a lockable door between one compartment and the adjacent one so, if there are four of you travelling together, you can make one compartment out of two, if you wish. They're usually very clean. What you cannot do is lock the door of your compartment from the outside when you go for meals.

Second class consists of four-berth compartments with a washbasin and drinking water supply. Third class is seats only. Sexes are separated in 1st and 2nd class unless you book the whole compartment. Again, compartments are not lockable from the outside, so never leave anything valuable lying around, and it's not a bad idea to padlock your rucksack to something.

Third class can get a little wearing on the nerves on long journeys, especially if they are overnight (which most are). Second class is more than adequate in this respect and 1st class is definitely a touch of luxury as far as budget travel goes.

You must book in advance for both 1st and 2nd class – two

DAWN DELANEY

Decorative gourds and childrens' toys, Nairobi Market

to three days is usually sufficient – otherwise you'll probably find that there are no berths available and you will have to go 3rd class. Visa credit cards are accepted for railway bookings.

Most trains have a dining car which provides dinner and breakfast. Meals are included in the price of the ticket but generally they're nothing special and the level of service is usually mediocre.

Bedding is provided in 1st and 2nd class and is also included in the ticket price.

Road

Kenyan roads are generally in good condition and many are excellent. The main exception to this is the Mombasa to Malaba road via Nairobi (the A109/104). This is the main road through the country and it not only takes Kenyan traffic but all of the heavy trucks bound for Uganda, Rwanda, Burundi and eastern Zaïre so it takes a constant battering. There are many long excellent sections but, equally, there are others in need of repair – especially between Nairobi and Mombasa. If a

truck forces you off the road along one of its narrow sections, you can virtually say goodbye to your entire suspension and, possibly, your life. Drive very carefully along this road and at all costs avoid driving at night.

The roads in the north and north-east and in the national parks are all gravel and usually in a reasonable state of repair, though there are long sections of corrugated gravel in some parts. Travelling on these can be agony on your kidneys after several hours, especially if you are on a bus which has had a double set of unyielding springs fitted to it.

If you're bringing your own vehicle to Kenya you should get a free three-month permit at the border on entry, so long as you have a valid *carnet de passage* for it. If you don't have a carnet you should be able to get a free one-week permit at the border on entry after which you must get an 'authorisation permit for a foreign private vehicle' at Nyayo House, Kenyatta Ave, Nairobi, which costs a few dollars but a lot of time queuing. Before you do this,

DAWN DELANEY

Fishermen untangle nets in the coastal town of Malindi

however, get in touch with the Automobile Association of Kenya which is in the Hurlingham shopping centre (sign-posted) in Nairobi.

When you are driving your own vehicle there are certain routes in north-east Kenya where you must obtain police permission before setting out. This is just a formality but there will be a roadblock to enforce this. The main stretch where this applies is between Isiolo and Marsabit where all transport must travel in convoy at a particular time of day unless you're turning off to go somewhere else (such as Samburu National Park, Wamba or Maralal).

Foreign-registered vehicles with a seating capacity of more than six people are not allowed into Kenyan game parks and reserves. The regulation is in force mainly to keep out the overland trucks.

Hiring a vehicle to tour Kenya (or at least the national parks) is a relatively expensive way of seeing the country but it does give you freedom of movement and is sometimes the only way of getting to the more remote parts of the country. On the other hand, if you're sharing costs, it's quite a feasible option.

Consult as many hire-charge leaflets as you can get hold of and a distances table before picking a hire company. When choosing a vehicle, be aware that at times other than the rainy season, a 2WD may be perfectly adequate in some parts of the country including Masai Mara Game Reserve, Amboseli and Tsavo national parks (at least on the main access routes of the latter), but it won't get you to the east side of Lake Turkana and would restrict your movements in the Aberdare and Meru national parks and the Buffalo Springs and Samburu game reserves. Most companies also have a policy of insisting that you take a 4WD if you're going upcountry and off the beaten track.

Bicycle

Bicycles are basically only in use in cities and there's not many of them. Virtually everyone travels by matatu. Anybody foolish enough to risk cycling along main roads in Kenya must be taking suicide seriously. It's safer to cycle in the countryside off the main roads. Always assume that the vehicle approaching you from behind is going to knock you off the road

so get off it before it reaches you. This obviously makes cycling tedious but it is better than ending up on a mortuary slab.

The hills of Kenya are not particularly steep but can be long and hard. You can expect to cover around 80 km per day in the hills of the western highlands, somewhat more where the country is flatter. Be wary of cycling off-road as punctures from thorn trees are a major problem.

Boat

Ferries operate in the Kenyan corner of Lake Victoria. These boats connect Kisumu with Kendu Bay and Homa Bay, and Homa Bay with Mfangano Island, but services are limited.

One of Kenya's most worthwhile and memorable experiences is sailing along the East African coast on a dhow. Many of the smaller dhows these days have been fitted with outboard motors so that progress can be made when there's no wind; the larger dhows are all motorised and some of them don't even have sails. Dhows can be picked up in Lamu but there are also possibilities in Mombasa.

Comment Circuler au Kenya

Bus

Le Kenya dispose d'un réseau de bus réguliers, de matatus (généralement des minibus), de taxis collectifs et de taxis privés traditionnels. Le mode de transport le plus économique est le bus, suivi du matatu, puis du taxi collectif (Peugeot) et, enfin, du taxi privé. Un trajet n'est guère plus long en bus qu'en matatu : la différence entre ces deux modes de transport se situe plutôt au niveau du risque.

Les compagnies de bus sont toutes privées, à une exception près. Certaines possèdent des véhicules en meilleur état que d'autres. Ainsi, le réseau d'Akamba Bus Service, le plus étendu, arrive premier au palmarès de la sécurité. KBS Stagecoach, la société nationale, assure elle aussi de nombreuses liaisons entre les grandes villes dans des bus modernes (dont plusieurs à étage) et fiables. Parmi les autres compagnies, Coastline, Goldline et Malindi sont correctes. Il existe dans certaines villes des sortes de "gares routières", qui se résument souvent à des zones mal définies et mal entretenues. Ailleurs, chaque compagnie possède son propre terminus, généralement proches les uns des autres. Dans la plupart des cas, les stations de matatus et de taxis collectifs se situent dans le même secteur. Par ailleurs, quelques "navettes" privées relient Nairobi à Mombasa et à Arusha et Moshi, en Tanzanie. Plus confortables que les bus, elles limitent à 18 le nombre de passagers et coûtent deux à trois fois plus cher.

Matatu

Les Kényans voyagent surtout en matatu, un mot qui signifie "trois" (au départ, un trajet en matatu coûtait trois pièces). Il peut aussi bien s'agir d'une vieille 504 Peugeot rafistolée dotée d'une remorque, que d'un minibus à 20 places flambant neuf avec installation stéréo, comme on en trouve à Nairobi. La plupart des trajets longues distances s'effectuent toutefois à bord de minibus Nissan blancs. Soumis aux pressions de leurs patrons, les chauffeurs visent un rendement maximal : ils conduisent vite, ignorent le mot "prudence" et ont tendance à surcharger leur véhicule. Ils n'hésitent pas non plus à prolonger leurs journées de travail. Il n'est pas étonnant, dans ces conditions, que les journaux regorgent de récits d'accidents de matatus, qui font chaque jour des morts et des blessés. Bien sûr, ce mode de transport représente parfois le seul moyen d'aller d'un point à un autre, mais évitez-le si vous avez le choix. Sachez que la route reliant Mombasa à Nairobi est réputée pour ses accidents.

Comme dans la plupart des pays d'Afrique de l'Est, on trouve toujours un matatu pour se rendre dans la ville la plus proche, voire plus loin s'il n'est pas trop tard. Il suffit d'interroger les chauffeurs aux terminus de bus. Les matatus partent une fois pleins et leurs tarifs sont fixes. Il est rare que l'on fasse payer plus cher aux étrangers.

DAVID ELSE

Mt Kenya – the Naro Moro route

Train

Les Kényans aiment voyager en train, même si les wagons, voies ferrées et autres infrastructures essentielles sont dans un état de délabrement avancé. Les trains partent à l'heure et sont bien plus sûrs que le bus ou le matatu. La ligne principale relie Mombasa, sur la côte, à Malaba, sur la frontière de l'Ouganda, en passant par Voi, Nairobi, Nakuru et Eldoret. Plusieurs voies secondaires effectuent les liaisons Nakuru-Kisumu, Nairobi-Nanyuki, Gilgil-Nyahururu, Voi-Taveta et Eldoret-Kitale. Des trains internationaux circulent également entre Nairobi et Kampala (Ouganda) via Malaba, et entre Voi et Moshi (Tanzanie) via Taveta, avec un aller-retour hebdomadaire pour chacun.

Il existe trois catégories de prix. En 1re classe, les compartiments renferment deux couchettes, un lavabo, un réservoir d'eau potable et un placard ; un service de bar est assuré. Les compartiments communiquent entre eux par une porte habituellement verrouillée, que l'on peut laisser ouverte quand on voyage à quatre. En général, la 1re classe est d'une propreté irréprochable. En 2e classe, les compartiments comprennent quatre couchettes, un lavabo et une réserve d'eau potable. On voyage assis en 3e classe. Hommes et femmes sont séparés en 1re et en 2e classes, à moins de réserver tout un compartiment. On ne peut verrouiller son compartiment de l'extérieur ; n'y laissez donc aucun objet de valeur si vous allez, par exemple, au wagon-restaurant. Il peut être judicieux d'attacher votre sac à dos quelque part au moyen d'un cadenas. Les longs voyages en 3e classe se révèlent souvent pénibles, surtout de nuit (presque tous les trajets sont nocturnes). La 2e classe, en revanche, est confortable. Quant à la 1re, elles entre dans la catégorie luxe selon les critères des voyageurs à petit budget ! Pensez à réservez pour les voyages en 1re et 2e classes (deux à trois jours suffisent), facilement complètes. Sans cette précaution, vous risquez de vous retrouver en 3e. On peut régler ses billets en carte Visa. La plupart des trains disposent d'un wagon-restaurant qui assure petit déjeuner et dîner. Ces repas sont en effet inclus dans le prix du billet, mais la qualité et le service laissent à désirer. Draps et couvertures sont fournis, sans supplément, en 1re et 2e classes.

Route

Le réseau routier est en bon état, beaucoup de routes se révèlent même excellentes. L'exception est la liaison Mombasa-Malaba via Nairobi (A109/104), l'axe principal du pays qu'empruntent non seulement les véhicules kényans, mais aussi les poids lourds qui desservent l'Ouganda, le Rwanda, le Burundi et l'est du Zaïre. Autant dire que la circulation est permanente. Certes, plusieurs tronçons sont en parfait état, mais les autres nécessiteraient d'importantes rénovations (en particulier la partie entre Nairobi et Mombasa). Sur l'une de ces sections étroites, un camion arrivant en face peut vous contraindre à faire une embardée et à quitter la route : vous pourrez alors dire adieu à vos suspensions ... et à la vie. Faites preuve d'une extrême prudence et ne roulez surtout pas de nuit.

Dans le nord et le nord-est du pays, ainsi que dans les parcs nationaux, on ne trouve que des routes à gravillons. Elles sont dans un état correct, à l'exception de longues sections à la surface inégale. Après plusieurs heures passées sur ces routes, votre dos demandera grâce, surtout si vous voyagez dans un bus aux suspensions rigides !

Si vous arrivez au Kenya au volant de votre propre véhicule, il vous faut un permis. Celui-ci, d'une durée de trois mois, est délivré gratuitement à la frontière sur présentation d'un carnet de passage en bonne et due forme. Sans ce dernier, vous n'obtiendrez qu'un permis d'une semaine et devrez ensuite réclamer une "autorisation pour véhicule privé étranger" auprès de la Nyayo House, Kenyatta Avenue, à Nairobi. Le coût de cette autorisation ne dépasse pas quelques dollars, mais il faut faire la queue pendant des heures. Pour éviter cette file d'attente, on peut toujours tenter sa chance à l'Automobile Association of Kenya, située au centre commercial de Hurlingham (signalé par des pancartes), à Nairobi.

Par ailleurs, certaines routes du nord-est ne sont accessibles aux véhicules individuels qu'après obtention d'un permis spécial délivré par la police. Il s'agit d'une simple formalité, que la présence de barrages à l'entrée de ces routes rend toutefois incontournable. Cette règle concerne en particulier le tronçon Isiolo-Marsabit, sur lequel les véhicules voyagent en convoi à une heure déterminée, sauf ceux qui ne l'empruntent que sur quelques kilomètres pour bifurquer ensuite vers une autre destination (comme le parc national de Samburu, Wamba ou Maralal).

L'entrée des réserves est interdite aux véhicules de plus de six places immatriculés à l'étranger, une règle qui vise surtout à éviter l'afflux de transporteurs routiers internationaux.

La location d'une voiture individuelle revient assez cher, mais représente le meilleur moyen de visiter le pays en toute liberté. C'est en effet la seule façon d'explorer certaines régions reculées. Si l'on partage les frais, cette solution est accessible aux budgets modestes. Comparez les prix et étudiez bien les distances avant d'opter pour tel ou tel loueur. Pour choisir le type de véhicule, sachez qu'en dehors de la saison des pluies, on peut parfaitement visiter certaines parties du Kenya comme la réserve de Masai Mara ou les parcs nationaux d'Amboseli et de Tsavo (à condition, pour ce dernier, d'emprunter la principale route d'accès) avec une voiture traditionnelle à deux roues motrices. En revanche, un véhicule 4x4 se révèle indispensable pour parcourir la rive orientale du lac Turkana, et préférable pour les parcs nationaux d'Aberdare et de Meru, ainsi que pour les réserves de Buffalo Springs et de Samburu. Quoi qu'il en soit, la plupart des sociétés de location refuseront de vous louer autre chose qu'un 4x4 si vous vous rendez dans le nord ou entendez sortir des sentiers battus.

Bicyclette

Assez rare au Kenya, la bicyclette n'est utilisée qu'en ville. Pour les longues distances, les gens préfèrent le matutu. Circuler à vélo sur une grande route équivaut à signer son arrêt de mort. Si le suicide n'entre pas dans vos projets, mieux vaut rouler à travers la campagne que sur la route. Partez toujours du principe que le véhicule qui arrive derrière vous va vous percuter et quittez la route avant qu'il vous rejoigne. Ce réflexe nécessaire rend les déplacements en bicyclette assez pénibles.

Les collines du Kenya ne sont pas particulièrement abruptes, mais leur ascension peut se révéler longue et difficile. Comptez 80 km par jour dans les hautes terres de l'ouest, un peu plus dans les régions moins accidentées. Soyez prudent si vous quittez la route : les épines des arbres provoquent des crevaisons.

Bateau

Un service de ferries est assuré sur la partie kényane du lac Victoria. Ces bateaux, assez peu fréquents, relient Kisumu à Kendu Bay et Homa Bay, et Homa Bay à l'île de Mfangano.

Autre expérience, plus intéressante et assurément mémorable : longer la côte est de l'Afrique à bord d'un boutre (voilier arabe). Même les plus petits d'entre eux sont souvent équipés d'un moteur, qui leur permet de se passer de vent. Les grands, eux, sont tous motorisés (certains ont même renoncé aux voiles). Ces bateaux se louent surtout à Lamu, mais aussi quelquefois à Mombasa.

DAVID ELSE

Zebras are one of the most common animals in the Kenyan Parks

Reisen in Kenia

Bus

In Kenia gibt es ein Netz aus regulären Bussen, Matatus (im allgemeinen Minibusse), Gemeinschaftstaxis und normalen Privattaxis. Die preiswerteste Reiseform ist der Bus, gefolgt von Matatu, Gemeinschaftstaxis (Peugeot Dienste) und zuletzt dem Privattaxi (teuer). Der Unterschied in Reisezeit zwischen normalen Bussen und Matatus ist unwesentlich, dafür ist der Unterschied in Sicherheit gravierend.

Mit einer Ausnahme sind alle Busunternehmen privat organisiert. Manche setzen jedoch bessere Busse ein als andere. Akamba Busdienst hat das umfassendste Netz und weist eine ziemlich gute Sicherheitsstatistik auf. Die staatliche Buslinie KBS Stagecoach setzt moderne Busse, inklusive einiger Doppeldecker, zu den wesentlichen Städten ein und ist ebenfalls zuverlässig und sicher. Von den anderen Privatunternehmen sind noch Coastline, Goldline und Malindi Bus in Ordnung.

In einigen Städten in Kenia gibt es so etwas ähnliches wie eine Bushaltestelle, was allerdings meist nicht mehr als eine Schmutzstelle ist. In anderen Orten hat jedes Busunternehmen seinen eigenen Terminal, doch sind diese oft nahe beieinander. Matatu und Gemeinschaftstaxi-Linien benutzen manchmal die gleichen Haltestellen wie Busse, was allerdings nicht immer der Fall ist.

Darüber hinaus gibt es noch eine Reihe privater "Pendelbusse", welche Nairobi mit Mombasa und mit Arusha und Moshi in Tansania verbinden. Sie sind komfortabler als die gewöhnlichen Busse, da sie nur etwa 18 Fahrgäste befördern. Dafür sind sie mindestens zwei bis dreimal so teuer wie die normalen Busse.

Matatu

Die meisten Einheimischen reisen per Matatu, was "drei" bedeutet (in den Anfängen der Matatus kostete die Fahrt drei Münzen). Diese können alle möglichen Formen haben, angefangen von kleinen, klapprigen Peugeot 504 Kleintransportern mit einer Kabine auf der Ladefläche, bis hin zu glänzenden, leuchtend bemalten 20-Sitzer Minibussen, komplett mit Megadezibel Stereoanlagen, wie man sie in Nairobi findet. Die Mehrzahl derjenigen, die Langstrecken bedienen, sind jedoch weiße Nissan Minibusse. Die meisten Matatu Fahrer stehen unter großem Druck von seiten ihrer Arbeitgeber, die Einnahmen zu maximieren. Daher tendieren sie dazu, rücksichtslos zu fahren und ihre Fahrzeuge zu überladen. Sie haben außerdem einen langen Arbeitstag. Täglich kann man in den Zeitungen Berichte über Matatu Unfälle finden, bei denen es viele Tote oder Verletzte gab. Natürlich benutzen viele Reisende Matatus und in manchen Fällen gibt es keine Alternative. Aber wenn es eine gibt (wie Bus oder Zug), sollte man diese vorziehen. Die Straße von Mombasa nach Nairobi ist berüchtigt wegen der Unfälle.

Wie in den meisten ostafrikanischen Ländern findet man immer einen Matatu, der in die nächste Stadt oder noch weiter fährt - vorausgesetzt es ist nicht zu spät am Tage. Am besten fragt man sich bei den Fahrern am Busparkplatz durch. Matatus fahren ab sobald sie voll sind und die Fahrpreise sind fix. Es ist unwahrscheinlich, daß man mehr bezahlen muß als die Einheimischen.

Zug

Kenias Eisenbahnen sind eine sehr beliebte Reiseform, trotz der Tatsache, daß die eingesetzten Wagen, die Schienen und andere wichtige Anlagen vernachläßigt worden sind. Die Züge sind im allgemeinen pünktlich und bedeutend sicherer als das Reisen per Bus oder Matatu. Die Haupteisenbahnlinie verläuft von Mombasa entlang der Küste nach Malaba an der Grenze zu Uganda über Voi, Nairobi, Nakuru und Eldoret, mit Nebenlinien von Nakuru nach Kisumu, Nairobi nach Nanyuki, Gilgil nach Nyahururu, Voi nach Taveta und von Eldoret nach Kitale.

Daneben gibt es noch internationale Linien zwischen Nairobi und Kampala (Uganda) über Malaba und zwischen Voi und Moshi (Tansania) über Taveta. Auf beiden Strecken gibt es eine Zugverbindung pro Woche je Richtung.

Kenias Eisenbahnen führen drei Klassen. Die Erste Klasse besteht aus Zweibett-Abteilen mit Waschbecken, Trinkwasser, Garderobe und Getränkeservice. Die Tür zwischen angrenzenden Abteilen ist abschließbar, so daß man, wenn man zu viert reist, zwei Abteile zu einem verbinden kann, wenn man will. Sie sind normalerweise sehr sauber. Man kann allerdings die Tür des Abteils nicht von außen abschließen, wenn man zum Essen geht.

Die Zweite Klasse besteht aus Vierbett-Abteilen mit Waschbecken und Trinkwasservorrat. In der Dritten Klasse gibt es nur Sitzplätze. In der Ersten und Zweiten Klasse sind die Geschlechter getrennt, es sei denn man bucht ein ganzes Abteil. Zur Erinnerung, die Abteile sind nicht von außen abschließbar, so daß man nie Wertsachen herumliegen lassen sollte. Es ist keine schlechte Idee, seinen Rucksack mit einem durch das Land und nimmt nicht nur Kenias Verkehr auf sondern auch noch all die Schwerlastwagen mit Ziel Uganda, Ruanda, Burundi und Ostzaire, so daß sie ständig stark beansprucht wird. Es gibt viele lange Strecken, die ausgezeichnet sind, aber auch genauso andere Strecken, die in reparaturbedürftigen Zustand sind, besonders zwischen Nairobi und Mombasa. Wenn man auf einer der engen Teilstrecken dieser Straße von einem LKW abgedrängt wird, kann man sich praktisch von seiner gesamten Federung verabschieden und, eventuell, von seinem Leben. Man sollte sehr vorsichtig auf dieser Straße fahren und es auf jeden Fall vermeiden, nachts unterwegs zu sein.

Die Straßen im Norden und Nordosten und in den Nationalparks sind Schotterstraßen und normalerweise in einem akzeptablen Zustand. Teilweise gibt es jedoch lange Strecken mit Querrillen im Schotter. Das Fahren auf diesen Strecken kann nach einigen Stunden zur Qual für die Nieren werden, besonders wenn man in einem Bus sitzt, der furchtbar schlecht gefedert ist.

Wenn man das eigene Auto nach Kenia mitnimmt, sollte man sich bei der Einreise an der Grenze eine kostenlose Dreimonats-Zulassung besorgen. Voraussetzung hierfür ist, daß man einen gültigen Zollpassierschein (carnet de passage) vorweisen kann. Wenn man keinen Passierschein hat, sollte es möglich sein, eine kostenlose einwöchige Zulassung an der Einreisegrenze zu bekommen. Mit dieser muß man sich dann einen "Genehmigungspassierschein für ein ausländisches Privatfahrzeug" beim Nyayo Haus, Kenyatta Ave, Nairobi, besorgen. Dieser kostet nur ein paar Dollar aber dafür viel Zeit beim Schlangestehen. Vorher sollte man sich jedoch mit der Automobile Association of

The Maasai – symbol of 'tribal' Kenya

DAVID ELSE

Vorhängeschloß an irgend etwas anzuschließen.

Die Dritte Klasse kann auf langen Strecken ein bißchen mühsam werden, besonders bei Nachtfahrten (was meist der Fall ist). Die Zweite Klasse ist mehr als angemessen in dieser Hinsicht und die Erste Klasse hat zweifellos einen Hauch von Luxus unter Billigreise-Maßstäben.

Für Erste und Zweite Klasse sollte man im voraus buchen – zwei bis drei Tage genügen im Allgemeinen – andernfalls wird man wahrscheinlich keine freien Betten mehr bekommen und muß dann Dritter Klasse fahren. Visa wird bei Eisenbahnbuchungen akzeptiert.

Die meisten Züge führen einen Speisewagen, welcher Abendessen und Frühstück anbietet. Die Mahlzeiten sind im Fahrpreis eingeschlossen, aber es ist normalerweise nichts Besonderes und der Service ist meist mittelmäßig.

Das Bettzeug wird in der Ersten und Zweiten Klasse bereitgestellt und ist ebenfalls im Fahrpreis inbegriffen.

Straße

Die Straßen in Kenia sind im allgemeinen in gutem Zustand, viele sind hervorragend. Die große Ausnahme ist die Straße von Mombasa nach Malaba über Nairobi (die A 109/104). Sie ist die Hauptverbindung

ROGER JONES

Giraffes graze mainly on acacia tree foliage in the early morning and afternoon

Kenya (Automobilvereinigung Kenia) in Verbindung setzen, welche sich im Hurlingham Einkaufszentrum (ausgeschildert) in Nairobi befindet.

Wenn man mit dem eigenen Fahrzeug unterwegs ist, muß man auf bestimmten Strecken in Nordost Kenia eine Polizeierlaubnis einholen, bevor man sich auf den Weg macht. Es ist zwar nur eine Formalität, doch gibt es eine Straßensperre um sie durchzusetzen. Die Hauptstrecke mit dieser Regelung verläuft zwischen Isiolo und Marsabit, wo der gesamte Verkehr zu bestimmten Tageszeiten im Konvoi fahren muß. Es sei denn, man biegt ab, um woanders hinzufahren (wie zum Samburu National Park, Wamba oder Maralal).

Im Ausland zugelassene Fahrzeuge mit einer Sitzkapazität von mehr als sechs Personen sind in Kenias Wildparks und Reservaten nicht gestattet. Diese Regelung ist vor allem in Kraft damit die Überland-Lastwagen draußen bleiben.

Um Kenia (oder zumindest die Nationalparks) zu bereisen ist das Mieten eines Autos ein relativ teurer Weg das Land

kennenzulernen. Es gibt einem aber Bewegungsfreiheit und ist manchmal die einzige Art, in etwas abgelegenere Ecken des Landes zu gelangen. Andererseits, wenn man sich die Kosten teilen kann, ist es durchaus eine machbare Alternative.

Man sollte so viele Preislisten von Autovermietungen wie möglich und eine Entfernungstabelle zu Rate ziehen, bevor man sich für ein Unternehmen entscheidet. Bei der Auswahl des Fahrzeuges sollte man daran denken, daß außerhalb der Regenzeit ein konventionelles Fahrzeug genau richtig ist für manche Landesteile, inklusive Masai Mara Wildreservat, Amboseli und Tsavo Nationalparks (zumindest auf den Hauptstraßen des letzteren). Aber es wird nicht ausreichen, um auf die Ostseite des Turkana Sees zu kommen und würde das Fahren im Aberdare und Meru Nationalpark wie auch in den Buffalo Springs und Samburu Wildreservaten einschränken. Die meisten Unternehmen bestehen außerdem grundsätzlich auf ein Geländefahrzeug, wenn man landeinwärts und außerhalb der ausgetretenen Wege fährt.

Fahrrad

Fahrräder werden im Grunde nur in Städten benutzt und es gibt nicht viele. Praktisch jeder fährt Matatu. Derjenige, der verrückt genug ist, das Risiko einzugehen, mit dem Fahrrad entlang der Hauptstraßen in Kenia zu fahren, spielt ernsthaft mit dem Gedanken Selbstmord zu begehen. Es ist sicherer auf dem Lande abseits der Hauptstraßen Fahrradzufahren. Man muß immer damit rechnen, von einem von hinten herannahenden Fahrzeug von der Straße gestoßen zu werden. Also fährt man besser selbst runter, bevor es einen erwischt. Das macht Fahrradfahren offensichtlich ermüdend, aber es ist immer noch besser als im Leichenschauhaus zu enden.

Die Hügel in Kenia sind nicht besonders steil, können aber lang und anstrengend sein. Man kann davon ausgehen, 80 km am Tag in den Hügeln des westlichen Hochlandes zurückzulegen, etwas mehr, wo das Land flacher ist. Beim Fahrradfahren abseits der Straße sollte man aufpassen, da Platten von Dornenbäumen ein großes Problem darstellen.

Boot

In der keniatischen Ecke des Viktoriasees verkehren Fähren. Diese Schiffe verbinden Kisumu mit der Kendu Bucht und Homa Bucht, sowie die Homa Bucht mit der Mfangano Insel. Die Betriebszeiten sind jedoch begrenzt.

Eines der besten Erlebnisse in Kenia, woran man sich lange erinnern wird, ist das Segeln auf einer Dhau entlang der ostafrikanischen Küste. Viele der kleineren Dhaus sind heutzutage mit einem Außenbordmotor ausgestattet, so daß man auch bei Flaute vorwärts kommt. Die größeren Dhaus sind alle motorisiert und einige haben nicht einmal Segel. Dhaus kann man in Lamu anmieten, es gibt dazu aber auch Möglichkeiten in Mombasa.

Cómo Movilizarse dentro de Kenia

En Autobús

Kenia tiene una red de autobuses regulares, matatus (normalmente microbuses), taxis colectivos y taxis privados ordinarios. El medio de trans-porte más barato es el autobús, luego siguen el matatu, los taxis colectivos (servicios Peugeot) y, por último, los taxis privados (que son caros). No existe mayor diferencia en cuanto al tiempo de transporte entre los autobuses ordinarios y los matatus, pero la diferencia en seguridad es enorme.

Todas las compañías de autobuses, excepto una, son privadas, pero algunas de ellas tienen mejores autobuses que las otras. El Servicio de Autobuses Akamba tiene la red más completa y su seguridad es bastante buena. La línea de autobuses del gobierno, KBS Stagecoach, tiene autobuses modernos, inclusive algunos de dos pisos, que van a las poblaciones principales, y también es puntual y segura. De las otras compañías privadas, Coastline, Goldline y Malindi Bus son aceptables.

Algunas de las poblaciones de Kenia tienen lo que se podría llamar 'estación de autobuses', aunque esto muchas veces no es más que un pequeño terreno. En otras poblaciones, cada compañía de autobuses tiene su propio terminal, aunque estos a menudo quedan cerca el uno del otro. Los matatus y los taxis colectivos algunas veces usan estos mismos terminales de autobuses pero no siempre es así.

También existe un número de 'autobuses de conexión' privados que unen a Nairobi con Mombasa y con Arusha y Moshi en Tanzania. Estos son más cómodos que los autobuses ordinarios ya que sólo transportan aproximadamente 18 pasajeros, pero son por lo menos dos o tres veces más caros.

En Matatu

El matatu (que quiere decir tres porque cuando comenzaron a funcionar el costo del viaje era tres monedas) es la manera en que la mayoría de las personas locales viaja. Estos pueden comprender desde las deterioradas furgonetas Peugeot 504 con una cabina atrás, hasta los nuevos microbuses de 20 asientos pintados de colores brillantes que incluyen estéreos de volumen a megadecibeles, como los que se encuentran en Nairobi. La mayoría de los que hacen los recorridos largos son los microbuses blancos Nissan. La mayoría de los conductores de matatu están bajo gran presión por parte de sus patronos para rendir buenas ganancias y por eso tienden a manejar de manera negligente y a sobrecargar los vehículos. También trabajan jornadas diarias demasiado largas. En los periódicos se pueden leer todos los días relatos de choques de matatus en los que muchas personas resultan muertas o heridas. Naturalmente que muchos viajeros los utilizan y, en algunos casos, no hay ninguna alternativa pero, cuando la haya (por ejemplo el autobús o el tren) es preferible utilizarlos. La carretera entre Mombasa y Nairobi es famosa por los choques.

Como en cualquier otro país del Africa Oriental, siempre se puede encontrar un matatu que viaja hacia la población siguiente, y aún más allá, siempre y cuando no sea demasiado tarde. Simplemente pregunte a los conductores que se encuentren estacionados. Los matatus parten cuando se llenan y los boletos tienen precio fijo. Es improbable que le pidan más de lo que pagan los pasajeros de la localidad.

En Tren

Los trenes son una forma muy popular de transporte en Kenia, a pesar de que el material rodante, las ferrovías y otras obras esenciales se han dejado deteriorar. Los trenes generalmente son puntuales y son mucho más seguros que los autobuses y los matatus. La vía férrea principal va desde Mombasa, en la costa de Malaba en la frontera entre Kenia y Uganda, pasando por Voi, Nairobi, Nakuru y Eldoret con líneas

HUGH FINLAY

Trash and Treasure – Kenyan style

secundarias que van de Nakuru a Kisumu, de Nairobi a Nayuki, de Gilgil a Niahururu, de Voi a Taveta y de Eldoret a Kitale.

También hay servicios internacionales entre Nairobi y Kampala (en Uganda) pasando por Malaba y entre Voi y Moshi (en Tanzania) pasando por Taveta. En ambas rutas, sale un tren cada semana en ambas direcciones.

En Kenia los trenes tienen tres clases de asientos. La primera clase consiste en cabinas de dos camas con un lavabo, agua potable, un guardarropa y servicio de bebidas. Hay una puerta que se puede cerrar con llave entre una cabina y la adyacente, así que si se desea, cuando cuatro personas viajen juntas, se puede hacer una sola cabina de dos. Por lo general son muy limpios. Lo que no se puede hacer es cerrar la puerta de la cabina con llave desde afuera cuando se va a las comidas.

La segunda clase consiste en cabinas de cuatro camas con un lavabo y agua potable. La tercera clase solamente ofrece asientos. Los sexos son separados en la primera y la segunda clases, a menos que se reserve toda la cabina. De nuevo, las cabinas no se pueden cerrar con llave desde afuera, así que no debe dejarse nada de valor a la vista, y no es mala idea asegurar contra algo por medio de un candado el morral o la maleta de viaje.

La tercera clase puede cansar un poco el sistema nervioso en los viajes largos, especialmente si se viaja por la noche (lo que ocurre en la mayoría de los casos). La segunda clase es más que adecuada en este respecto y la primera clase es definitivamente un poco lujosa para los que quieran viajar económicamente.

Para la primera y la segunda clases se deben hacer las reservaciones por anticipado; por lo general dos o tres días

son suficientes, de lo contrario podría ser que no encontrara cabinas disponibles y entonces tendría que viajar en tercera clase. Las tarjetas de crédito Visa son aceptadas para las reservaciones de tren.

La mayoría de los trenes tienen un vagón comedor que ofrece cena y desayuno. Las comidas son incluidas en el precio del boleto pero, por lo general, no son nada especial y la calidad de servicio es generalmente mediocre.

En la primera y la segunda clases se suministra la ropa de cama, lo que está incluido en el precio del boleto.

Por Carretera

Las carreteras de Kenia están generalmente en buenas condiciones y muchas son excelentes. La excepción principal es la carretera de Mombasa a Malaba que pasa por Nairobi (la ruta A109/104). Esta es la carretera principal a través del país que no solamente toma el tráfico de Kenia sino todos los camiones pesados que van hacia Uganda, Rwanda, Burundi y Zaire oriental así que es maltratada constantemente. Hay muchas secciones largas en excelentes condiciones pero, igualmente, hay otras que necesitan reparación, especialmente entre Nairobi y Mombasa. Si un camión lo fuerza a uno a salirse de la carretera se puede uno despedir de la suspensión completa del vehículo, y quizás de la vida. Conduzca cautelosamente a lo largo de esta carretera y, a todo costo, evite conducir de noche.

Las carreteras del norte y del noreste y los parques nacionales son todas de grava pero generalmente en condiciones razonables, aunque hay largas secciones de grava corrugadas en algunas partes. El viajar por estas carreteras puede resultar en agonía para los riñones después de varias horas, especialmente si se viaja en un autobús

al que se le haya instalado un doble juego de amortiguadores que no amortiguan nada.

Si usted va a traer su propio vehículo a Kenia puede obtener un permiso gratuito de tres meses en la frontera de entrada, siempre y cuando tenga un *carnet de passage* válido para esto. Si no tiene un carné, puede que obtenga un permiso gratuito de una semana en la frontera de entrada. Después de esto, tendrá que obtener un 'permiso de autorización para vehículo privado extranjero' en la Nyayo House, Kenyatta Avenue, Nairobi, que cuesta unos pocos dólares pero por el que hay que esperar mucho tiempo en la cola. Sin embargo, antes de hacer esto, póngase en contacto con la Asociación Automobilista de Kenia (Automobile Association of Kenya) en Nairobi que está en el centro comercial Hurlingham (tiene aviso).

Al conducir su propio vehículo hay ciertas rutas en el noreste de Kenia para las que se tiene que obtener permiso policivo antes de salir. Esto es simplemente una formalidad y habrá bloqueos de carretera para exigirlos. La sección principal donde esto se exige es entre Isiolo y Marsabit por donde todo el transporte tiene que ir en convoy durante un período particular del día, a menos que se vire para dirigirse a otro lugar (como por ejemplo al Parque Nacional Samburu, a Wamba o a Maralal).

A los vehículos de registración extranjera con asientos para más de seis personas no se les permite entrar a los parques y reservas de animales. Esta regulación es principalmente para impedir la entrada de camiones de transporte.

El alquilar un vehículo para viajar por Kenia (o por lo menos por los parques nacionales) es una forma relativamente cara de ver el país, pero le ofrece a uno la libertad de movimiento y es algunas veces la única manera de visitar las partes más remotas del país. Por otra parte, si se está compartiendo los costos, esta es una opción bastante factible.

Antes de escoger la compañía de coches de alquiler consulte la mayor cantidad de folletos que pueda obtener y una tabla de distancias. Al escoger el vehículo, tenga en cuenta que en algunas ocasiones, excepto en las épocas de lluvia, un vehículo de tracción a dos ruedas (2WD) puede ser lo suficientemente adecuado para algunas partes del país, incluso la Reserva Animal Masai Mara, los parques nacionales Amboseli y Tsavo (por lo menos por las rutas principales de acceso de este último), pero no le llevará al lado oriental del Lago Turkana y restringirá sus movimientos en los parques nacionales Aberdare y Meru y en las reservas animales Buffalo Springs y Samburu. La mayoría de las compañías también tienen la política de insistir en que usted alquile un vehículo de tracción a cuatro ruedas (4WD) si va a viajar a la parte alta del país y fuera de las vías principales.

En Bicicleta

Básicamente, la bicicleta solamente se usa en las ciudades, y no se ven muchas. Virtualmente todo el mundo viaja en matatu. El que cometa la tontería de arriesgarse a viajar en bicicleta por las vías principales de Kenia, debe estar considerando el suicidio seriamente. Es más seguro viajar en bicicleta en el campo o por las vías secundarias. Siempre debe presumirse que el vehículo que se esté aproximando por detrás va a lanzarlo a uno fuera del camino, así que bájese antes de que lo alcance. Evidentemente esto hace el viaje tedioso pero es mucho mejor que terminar en la funeraria.

Las colinas no son particularmente pendientes pero pueden ser prolongadas y difíciles. Usted puede esperar recorrer aproximadamente 80 km al día en las colinas occidentales, un poco más donde el terreno sea plano. Tenga precaución de no salirse fuera de la carretera con la bicicleta pues los pinchazos debidos a ramas de árboles espinosos son un problema serio.

En Bote

El servicio de botes opera en el extremo del Lago Victoria que le pertenece a Kenia. Estos botes comunican a Kisumu con la Bahía Kendu y con la Bahía Homa; y la Bahía Homa con Mfangano; pero los servicios son limitados.

Una de las experiencias más memorables y que más valen la pena es navegar a lo largo de la Costa Este Africana en embarcación de vela de un solo mastil (dhow). Muchas de estas embarcaciones pequeñas han sido equipadas con motores fuera de borda para así poder continuar navegando cuando no haya viento; las más grandes todas han sido motorizadas y algunas de ellas ni siquiera tienen velas. Estas embarcaciones pueden tomarse en Lamu pero también es posible poder tomarlas en Mombasa.

Pink flamingos crowd the shores of Lake Elmenteita

ケニアの旅

バス

ケニアには定期バス、マタトゥ(matatu:通常はミニバス)、乗合タクシー、普通の個人タクシーなどの交通網がある。一番安い交通手段はバスで、マタトゥ、乗合タクシー(プジョー製)、個人タクシーの順に料金が高くなる。普通のバスとマタトゥの間には乗車時間に差はあまりないが、安全面では大きな違いがある。

バス会社は一社を除いてすべて私営だが、そのうちの数社は他社よりバスのコンディションがいい。アカンバ・バス・サービス(Akamba Bus Service)はもっとも広いネットワークを持ち、安全面でも比較的良い成績を上げている。政府のバス機関であるKBSステージコーチ社(KBS Stagecoach)は二階建てを含む近代的なバスで主要都市を結び、信頼性と安全性も高い。これ以外の私営バス会社のなかではコーストライン(Coastline)、ゴールドライン(Goldline)、マリンディ・バス(Malindi Bus)などがいい。

いくつかのケニアの町には「バス停」らしきものがあるが、だいたいは踏み固められた土の一画がそう呼ばれているにすぎない。そのほかの町にはバス会社がそれぞれ独自のターミナルを持っているが、互いに近くに集まっていることが多い。必ずというわけではないが、マタトゥと乗合タクシーはバスとおなじ停留所を使う。

このほかにもナイロビ(Nairobi)とモンバサ(Mombasa)、タンザニアのアルシャ(Arusha)、モーシ(Moshi)をつなぐ数多くの私営「シャトルバス」がある。これらは最高18人乗りなので普通のバスよりも乗り心地がいいが、料金は少なくとも2倍から3倍高い。

マタトゥ

地元の人々が最も多く利用するのが、数字の「3」という意味のマタトゥだ(マタトゥが運行しはじめたころはコイン3枚で乗れたから)。マタトゥの種類には、下は後部に客室がある小さくてぼろぼろの

プジョー504から、上はぴかぴかで派手に色付けし音楽をがんがんかけて走る、ナイロビでよく見かける20人乗りのミニバスまである。しかし長距離を走るもののほとんどは日産の白いミニバスだ。マタトゥの運転手は儲けを最大にするようにとの雇用主からのプレッシャーが大きいため無謀運転をしたり荷の積みすぎをする傾向があり、長時間労働をしがちだ。マタトゥの衝突事故で多くの怪我人や死亡者が出たという記事は毎日のように新聞に載る。もちろん旅行者も多く利用するし、ときにはほかに交通手段がないこともある。しかし、もしバスや電車など他の方法があるときはそれらを優先したほうがいい。モンバサーナイロビ間の道路は衝突事故が多いことで悪名高い。

多くの西アフリカ諸国のように、遅い時刻でなければ、隣町や遠くの田舎に向かうマタトゥをすぐに見つけることができる。バス停で運転手達に聞きまわりさえすればよい。マタトゥは満員になり次第発車し、料金は固定制だ。地元の乗客より料金を多く取られることはまずない。

電車

ケニヤの電車は、車両、鉄道、その他の基本的な設備が老朽化しているにもかかわらず、とても人気がある交通手段だ。電車は時刻どおりに運行し、バスやマタトゥよりもはるかに安全だ。幹線鉄道は海岸沿いのモンバサから、ヴォイ(Voi)、ナイロビ(Nairobi)、ナクール(Nakuru)、エルドレト(Eldoret)を経由して、ケニ

DAVID WALL

Leopards are one of the most widespread yet least observed of the big cats

Elephants – one of the 'Big 5' wildlife attractions to be seen in Kenya's parks

DAVID WALL

ヤとウガンダ国境のマラバ (Malaba) まで結んでおり、それ以外にナクールからキスム (Kisumu) まで、ナイロビからナニュク (Nanyuki) まで、ギルギル (Gilgil) からニャフルル (Nyahururu) まで、ヴォイからタヴェタ (Taveta) まで、エルドレト (Eldoret) からキタレ (Kitale) までの支線がある。

国際便として、マラバ経由でナイロビからウガンダのカンパラ (Kampala) まで行く線と、タヴェタ経由でヴォイからタンザニアのモシ (Moshi) まで行く線がある。どちらも上りと下り列車が週一便ずつ運行している。

ケニヤの電車の座席は 3 つの等級がある。一等席は寝台が 2 つの客室で、洗面台、飲料水、衣装箪笥、飲み物のサービスが付いている。隣り合

わせの客室の間には鍵がかかるドアがあるので、4 人で旅行する場合は客室二つを借り切って一つ分として使うこともできる。通常はとても清潔だ。しかし、食事などで客室を離れるときは客室の鍵を外からかけることはできない。

二等席は寝台が 4 つの客室で洗面台と飲料水がある。三等席は座席のみ。客室を借り切る以外は一、二等席とも男女別になっている。重ねて言うが、客室は外から鍵をかけられないので貴重品を出しっぱなしにせず、リュックサックを持ち出せないように南京錠で何かに固定しておくといい。

三等席は長距離旅行、とくに夜行（ほとんどの場合夜行）だと少々神経がくたびれるかもしれない。この点で言えば二等席は十分すぎるくらいで、

予算が許せば一等席は贅沢感を味わえる。

一、二等席はふつう 2, 3 日前に予約が必要。さもないと満席で、三等席に乗らないといけなくなる。列車の予約には Visa カードが使える。

ほとんどの列車には食堂車があり夕食と朝食がとれる。食事はチケット代に含まれているが食事は特にすばらしいわけではなくサービスも月並みだ。

寝具は用意されていて料金はチケット代に含まれている。

道路

ケニヤの道路は一般的にコンディションが良く、その多くはすばらしく良い。ところが例外的なものもある。その代表は、ナイロビ経由のモザンビーク－マラバ間道路（A109/104 号線）

だ。これは国内を貫く幹線道路で、ケニヤの輸送自動車だけでなく、ウガンダ、ルワンダ、ブルンディ、ザイール東部を結ぶすべての大型トラックが通るのでつねに傷んでいる。コンディションがとても良い区間もあるが、同時に修理が必要な部分もある。とくに、ナイロビーモンバサ間がそうだ。道が狭い部分でトラックに道から押し出されたら、サスペンションが全部だめになること、場合によっては命の保証もないことを覚悟すること。この道路を運転するときには十分注意し、夜間の運転は可能な限り避けること。

北部、北東部、国立公園内の道路はすべて砂利道で、満足いく程度に修理されてはいるが、長い区間にわたってがたがたのひどい砂利道という部分もある。数時間走ると腎臓が痛くなるほどだ。固めのサスペンションを通常の2倍使っているバスに乗った場合はとくにひどい。

ケニヤ国内に自家用車を持ち込むときは有効なカルネ(carnet de passage：車で通過するときの無関税許可証)があれば入国時に国境で3ヶ月有効許可証を無料で入手できる。カルネがない場合は、ナイロビのケニヤッタ通り(Kenyatta Ave)にあるニャヨ・ハウス(Nyayo House)で、外国自家用車認可証書(authorisation permit for a foreign private vehicle)を入手すれば(数ドルだが長時間待たされる)、入国時に国境で無料の1週間有効許可証を入手できるはずだ。その前にナイロビのハーリンガム・ショッピングセンター(Hurlingham shopping centre という看板がある)内にあるケニヤ自動車協会(Automobile Association of Kenya)と連絡をとること。

ケニヤ北西部には、自家用車を運転する際、出発前にあらかじめ警察の許可が必要なルートがいくつかある。単なる形式上のことだが、これを施行するための道路封鎖もある。おもな路線は、イシオロ(Isiolo)ーマーサビト(Marsabit)間で、途中で脇道にそれる(たとえばサンブル国立公園：Samburu National Park、ワンバ：Wamba、マララール：Maralalなどへ向かう)車以外はすべて一定の時刻に一団となって護送される。

7人乗り以上の外国登録車はケニヤの猟鳥獣保護公園および地域に乗り入れることはできない。これは陸上運送トラックの立ち入りを規制するためだ。

レンタカーでケニヤをツアーするのは比較的高くつく観光手段だが、自由に移動できるのが利点だ。また、遠隔地域に行くにはこの方法しかない。共同で借りるのなら実行可能だ。

レンタカー会社を決める前にできるだけ多くの料金表と走行距離表を比較検討すること。車種を選ぶ際、雨季以外ならマサイ・マラ猟鳥獣保護地域(Masai Mara Game Reserve)、アンボセリ国立公園(Amboseli National Park)、ツァヴォ国立公園(Tsavo National Park)などの地域は2WDで十分だが(ツァヴォ国立公園のおもな通路はまず大丈夫)、トゥルカナ湖(Lake Turkana)の東岸までは入れないし、アバデア国立公園(Aberdare National Park)、メル国立公園(Meru National Park)、バッファロー・スプリングス猟鳥獣保護地域(Buffalo Springs Game Reserve)、サンブル猟鳥獣保護地域(Samburu Game Reserve)などは2WDでは移動不可能な

地域がある。奥地に行く場合や踏み固められた道を外れる場合、レンタカー会社のほとんどが4WDを強く勧める。

自転車

自転車は数があまり多くなく、基本的に都市だけで使われている。人々はほとんどマタトゥで移動する。ケニヤの主要道路を自転車で移動するような無謀な真似をする人は本気で自殺を覚悟したほうがいい。主要道路を離れて田舎で自転車に乗るほうが安全だ。つねに後ろから来る車に轢かれることを予測して、車が近づいてきたら自転車から降りるようにすること。大変わずらわしいことだが、棺桶に入るよりはましだ。

ケニヤの坂はあまり急ではないが、長くてつらい。西部の高地では1日80キロメートルは丘が続くと考えていい。平地もこれよりいくぶんかましな程度。道から逸れるときは刺植物でパンクすることがよくあるので気をつけること。

ボート

ケニヤ側のビクトリア湖(Lake Victoria)にはフェリーが運行している。これらはキスム(Kisumu)とケンドゥ湾(Kendu Bay)、ホマ湾(Homa Bay)、また、ホマ湾(Homa Bay)とムファンガノ島(Mfangano Island)を結ぶが便数は少ない。

ケニヤの旅行でもっともすばらしい体験が味わえるものの一つは東アフリカ岸をダウ(帆船)で航行することだ。小型ダウのほとんどが船外モータ付きになったので風がないときでも進める。大型のダウはすべてモーター付きで、帆さえないものもある。ダウはラム(Lamu)で乗れるがモンバサでも乗れることがある。

DAVID ELSE

DAVID WALL

DAVID WALL

Left: Giant Lobelia
Top right: Lilac-Breasted Roller
Bottom right: Pelicans in flight, Lake Nakuru

Index

Note: Geographical and cultural features are also listed separately at the end of the general index in their appropriate categories.

GENERAL INDEX
All entries in Kenya except:

E - Ethiopia
S - Somalia
Su - Sudan
T - Tanzania
U - Uganda

LONELY PLANET PRODUCTS

AFRICA

Africa on a shoestring • Arabic (Moroccan) phrasebook • Cape Town city guide • Central Africa • East Africa • Egypt • Egypt trave atlas • Ethiopian (Amharic) phrasebook • Kenya • Kenya travel atlas • Morocco • North Africa • South Africa, Lesotho & Swaziland • South Africa, Lesotho & Swaziland travel atlas •Swahili phrasebook • Trekking in East Africa• West Africa • Zimbabwe, Botswana & Namibia • Zimbabwe, Botswana & Namibia travel atlas

Travel Literature: The Rainbird: A Central African Journey • Songs to an African Sunset: A Zimbabwean Story

ANTARCTICA

Antarctica

AUSTRALIA & THE PACIFIC

Australia • Australian phrasebook • Bushwalking in Australia • Bushwalking in Papua New Guinea • Fiji • Fijian phrasebook • Islands of Australia's Great Barrier Reef • Melbourne city guide • Micronesia • New Caledonia • New South Wales & the ACT • New Zealand • Northern Territory • Outback Australia • Papua New Guinea • Papua New Guinea phrasebook • Queensland • Rarotonga & the Cook Islands • Samoa • Solomon Islands • South Australia • Sydney city guide • Tahiti & French Polynesia • Tasmania • Tonga • Tramping in New Zealand • Vanuatu • Victoria • Western Australia

Travel Literature: Islands in the Clouds • Sean & David's Long Drive

CENTRAL AMERICA & THE CARIBBEAN

Bermuda • Central America on a shoestring • Costa Rica • Cuba • Eastern Caribbean • Guatemala, Belize & Yucatán: La Ruta Maya • Jamaica

EUROPE

Austria • Baltic States & Kaliningrad • Baltics States phrasebook • Britain • Central Europe on a shoestring • Central Europe phrasebook • Czech & Slovak Republics • Denmark • Dublin city guide • Eastern Europe on a shoestring • Eastern Europe phrasebook • Finland • France • Greece • Greek phrasebook • Hungary • Iceland, Greenland & the Faroe Islands • Ireland • Italy • Mediterranean Europe on a shoestring • Mediterranean Europe phrasebook • Paris city guide • Poland • Prague city guide • Russia, Ukraine & Belarus • Russian phrasebook • Scandinavian & Baltic Europe on a shoestring • Scandinavian Europe phrasebook • Slovenia • St Petersburg city guide • Switzerland • Trekking in Greece • Trekking in Spain • Ukrainian phrasebook • Vienna city guide • Walking in Switzerland • Western Europe on a shoestring • Western Europe phrasebook

INDIAN SUBCONTINENT

Bangladesh • Bengali phrasebook • Delhi city guide • Hindi/Urdu phrasebook • India • India & Bangladesh travel atlas • Indian Himalaya • Karakoram Highway • Nepal • Nepali phrasebook • Pakistan • Sri Lanka • Sri Lanka phrasebook • Trekking in the Indian Himalaya • Trekking in the Karakoram & Hindukush • Trekking in the Nepal Himalaya

Travel Literature: In Rajasthan • Shopping for Buddhas

ISLANDS OF THE INDIAN OCEAN

Madagascar & Comoros • Maldives & Islands of the East Indian Ocean • Mauritius, Réunion & Seychelles

MIDDLE EAST & CENTRAL ASIA

Arab Gulf States • Arabic (Egyptian) phrasebook • Central Asia • Iran • Israel & the Palestinian Territories • Israel & the Palestinian Territories travel atlas • Jordan & Syria • Jordan, Syria & Lebanon travel atlas • Middle East • Turkey • Turkish phrasebook • Yemen

Travel Literature: The Gates of Damascus • Kingdom of the Film Stars: Journey into Jordan

NORTH AMERICA

Alaska • Backpacking in Alaska • Baja California • California & Nevada • Canada • Florida • Hawaii • Honolulu city guide • Los Angeles city guide • Mexico • Miami city guide • New England • New Orleans city guide • Pacific Northwest USA • Rocky Mountain States • San Francisco city guide • Southwest USA • USA phrasebook

NORTH-EAST ASIA

Beijing city guide • Cantonese phrasebook • China • Hong Kong city guide • Hong Kong, Macau & Guangzhou • Japan • Japanese phrasebook • Japanese audio pack • Korea • Korean phrasebook • Mandarin phrasebook • Mongolia • Mongolian phrasebook • North-East Asia on a shoestring • Seoul city guide • Taiwan • Tibet • Tibet phrasebook • Tokyo city guide

Travel Literature: Lost Japan

SOUTH AMERICA

Argentina, Uruguay & Paraguay • Bolivia • Brazil • Brazilian phrasebook • Buenos Aires city guide • Chile & Easter Island • Chile & Easter Island travel atlas • Colombia • Ecuador & the Galápagos Islands • Latin American Spanish phrasebook • Peru • Quechua phrasebook • Rio de Janeiro city guide • South America on a shoestring • Trekking in the Patagonian Andes • Venezuela

Travel Literature: Full Circle: A South American Journey

SOUTH-EAST ASIA

Bali & Lombok • Bangkok city guide • Burmese phrasebook• Cambodia • Ho Chi Minh city guide • Indonesia • Indonesian phrasebook • Indonesian audio pack • Jakarta city guide • Java • Laos • Laos travel atlas • Lao phrasebook • Malaysia, Singapore & Brunei • Myanmar (Burma) • Philippines • Pilipino phrasebook • Singapore city guide • South-East Asia on a shoestring • South-East Asia phrasebook • Thailand • Thailand travel atlas • Thai phrasebook • Thai Hill Tribes phrasebook • Thai audio pack • Vietnam • Vietnamese phrasebook • Vietnam travel atlas

LONELY PLANET GUIDES TO AFRICA

Africa on a shoestring
From Marrakesh to Kampala, Mozambique to Mauritania, Johannesburg to Cairo – this guidebook has all the facts on travelling in Africa. Comprehensive information on more than 50 countries.

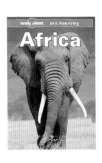

Arabic (Egyptian) phrasebook
This handy phrasebook is packed with words and phrases to cover almost every situation. Arabic script is included making this phrasebook useful to travellers in most other Arabic-speaking countries.

Arabic (Moroccan) phrasebook
Whether finding a hotel or asking for a meal, this indispensable phrasebook will help travellers to North Africa make their travels with ease. This phrasebook also includes Arabic script and a helpful pronunciation guide.

Cape Town city guide
Cape Town offers lively cafés, magnificent surf beaches and superb mountain walks. This indispensable guide is packed with insider tips for both business and leisure travellers.

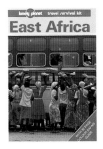

Central Africa
This guide tells where to go to meet gorillas in the jungle, how to catch a steamer down the Congo...even the best beer to wash down grilled boa constrictor! Covers Cameroun, the Central African Republic, Chad, the Congo, Equatorial Guinea, Gabon, São Tomé & Principe, and Zaïre.

East Africa
Detailed information on Kenya, Uganda, Rwanda, Burundi, eastern Zaïre and Tanzania. The latest edition includes a 32-page full-colour Safari Guide.

Egypt
This guide takes you into and beyond the spectacular and mysterious pyramids, temples, tombs, monasteries, mosques and bustling main streets of Egypt.

Ethiopian (Amharic) phrasebook
You'll enjoy Ethiopia a whole lot more if you can speak some of the language. All the phrases you need are at your fingertips in this handy phrasebook.

Kenya
This superb guide features a 32-page Safari Guide with colour photographs, illustrations and information on East Africa's famous wildlife.

Morocco
This thoroughly revised and expanded guide is full of down-to-earth information and reliable advice for every budget. It includes a 20-page colour section on Moroccan arts and crafts and information on trekking routes in the High Atlas and Rif Mountains.

North Africa
A most detailed and comprehensive guide to the Maghreb – Morocco, Algeria, Tunisia and Libya. It points the way to fascinating bazaars, superb beaches and the vast Sahara, and is packed with reliable advice for every budget. This new guide includes a 20-page full colour section on Moroccan arts and crafts.

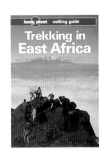

South Africa, Lesotho & Swaziland
Travel to southern Africa and you'll be surprised by its cultural diversity and incredible beauty. There's no better place to see Africa's amazing wildlife. All the essential travel details are included in this guide as well as information about wildlife reserves, and a 32-page full colour Safari Guide.

Swahili phrasebook
Swahili is a major lingua franca of the African continent. This handy phrasebook will prove invaluable for travellers to Africa.

Trekking in East Africa
Practical, first-hand information for trekkers for a region renowned for its spectacular national parks and rewarding trekking trails. Covers treks in Kenya, Tanzania, Uganda and Malawi.

West Africa
All the necessary information for independent travel in Benin, Burkino Faso, Cape Verde, Côte d'Ivoire, The Gambia, Ghana, Guinea, Guinea-Bissau, Liberia, Mali, Mauritania, Niger, Nigeria, Senegal, Sierra Leone and Togo. Includes a colour section on local culture and birdlife.

Zimbabwe, Botswana & Namibia
Exotic wildlife, breathtaking scenery and fascinating people...this comprehensive guide shows a wilder, older side of Africa for the adventurous traveller. Includes a 32-page colour Safari Guide.

LONELY PLANET TRAVEL ATLASES

Conventional fold-out maps work just fine when you're planning your trip on the kitchen table, but have you ever tried to use one – or the half-dozen you sometimes need to cover a country – while you're actually on the road? Even if you have the origami skills necessary to unfold the sucker, you know that flimsy bit of paper is not going to last the distance.

"Lonely Planet travel atlases are designed to make it through your journey in one piece – the sturdy book format is based on the assumption that since all travellers want to make it home without punctures, tears or wrinkles, the maps they use should too."

The travel atlases contain detailed, colour maps that are checked on the road by our travel authors to ensure their accuracy. Place name spellings are consistent with our associated guidebooks, so you can use the atlas and the guidebook hand in hand as you travel and find what you are looking for. Unlike conventional maps, each atlas has a comprehensive index, as well as a detailed legend and helpful 'getting around' sections translated into five languages. Sorry, no free steak knives...

Features of this series include:

- full-colour maps, plus colour photos
- maps researched and checked by Lonely Planet authors
- place names correspond with Lonely Planet guidebooks, so there are no confusing spelling differences
- complete index of features and place names
- atlas legend and travelling information presented in five languages: English, French, German, Spanish and Japanese

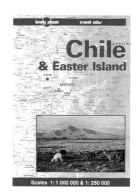

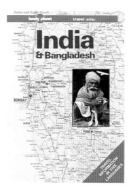

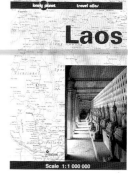

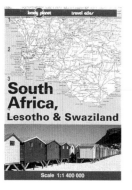

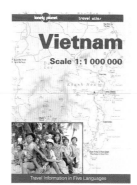

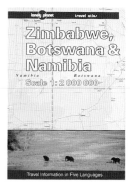

PLANET TALK

Lonely Planet's FREE quarterly newsletter

We love hearing from you and think you'd like to hear from us.

When...is the right time to see reindeer in Finland?
Where...can you hear the best palm-wine music in Ghana?
How...do you get from Asunción to Areguá by steam train?
What...is the best way to see India?

For the answer to these and many other questions read PLANET TALK.

Every issue is packed with up-to-date travel news and advice including:

- a letter from Lonely Planet co-founders Tony and Maureen Wheeler
- go behind the scenes on the road with a Lonely Planet author
- feature article on an important and topical travel issue
- a selection of recent letters from travellers
- details on forthcoming Lonely Planet promotions
- complete list of Lonely Planet products

To join our mailing list contact any Lonely Planet office.

Also available: Lonely Planet T-shirts. 100% heavyweight cotton.

LONELY PLANET ONLINE

Get the latest travel information before you leave or while you're on the road

Whether you've just begun planning your next trip, or you're chasing down specific info on currency regulations or visa requirements, check out the Lonely Planet World Wide Web site for up-to-the-minute travel information.

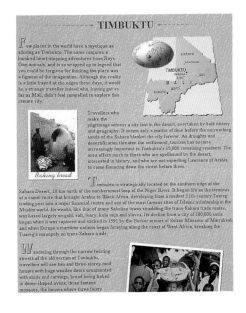

As well as travel profiles of your favourite destinations (including interactive maps and full-colour photos), you'll find current reports from our army of researchers and other travellers, updates on health and visas, travel advisories, and the ecological and political issues you need to be aware of as you travel.

There's an online travellers' forum (the Thorn Tree) where you can share your experiences of life on the road, meet travel companions and ask other travellers for their recommendations and advice. We also have plenty of links to other Web sites useful to independent travellers.

With tens of thousands of visitors a month, the Lonely Planet Web site is one of the most popular on the Internet and has won a number of awards including GNN's Best of the Net travel award.

http://www.lonelyplanet.com

THE LONELY PLANET STORY

Lonely Planet published its first book in 1973 in response to the numerous 'How did you do it?' questions Maureen and Tony Wheeler were asked after driving, bussing, hitching, sailing and railing their way from England to Australia.

Written at a kitchen table and hand collated, trimmed and stapled, *Across Asia on the Cheap* became an instant local bestseller, inspiring thoughts of another book.

Eighteen months in South-East Asia resulted in their second guide, *South-East Asia on a shoestring*, which they put together in a backstreet Chinese hotel in Singapore in 1975. The 'yellow bible', as it quickly became known to backpackers around the world, soon became *the* guide to the region. It has sold well over half a million copies and is now in its 8th edition, still retaining its familiar yellow cover.

Today there are over 180 titles, including travel guides, walking guides, language kits & phrasebooks, travel atlases and travel literature. The company is one of the largest travel publishers in the world. Although Lonely Planet initially specialised in guides to Asia, we now cover most regions of the world, including the Pacific, North America, South America, Africa, the Middle East and Europe.

The emphasis continues to be on travel for independent travellers. Tony and Maureen still travel for several months of each year and play an active part in the writing, updating and quality control of Lonely Planet's guides.

They have been joined by over 70 authors and 170 staff at our offices in Melbourne (Australia), Oakland (USA), London (UK) and Paris (France). Travellers themselves also make a valuable contribution to the guides through the feedback we receive in thousands of letters each year.

The people at Lonely Planet strongly believe that travellers can make a positive contribution to the countries they visit, both through their appreciation of the countries' culture, wildlife and natural features, and through the money they spend. In addition, the company makes a direct contribution to the countries and regions it covers. Since 1986 a percentage of the income from each book has been donated to ventures such as famine relief in Africa; aid projects in India; agricultural projects in Central America; Greenpeace's efforts to halt French nuclear testing in the Pacific; and Amnesty International.

'I hope we send people out with the right attitude about travel. You realise when you travel that there are so many different perspectives about the world, so we hope these books will make people more interested in what they see.'

– Tony Wheeler

LONELY PLANET PUBLICATIONS

AUSTRALIA (HEAD OFFICE)
PO Box 617, Hawthorn 3122, Victoria
tel: (03) 9819 1877   fax: (03) 9819 6459
e-mail: talk2us@lonelyplanet.com.au

UK
10 Barley Mow Passage,
Chiswick, London W4 4PH
tel: (0181) 742 3161   fax: (0181) 742 2772
e-mail: 100413.3551@compuserve.com

USA
Embarcadero West,155 Filbert St, Suite 251,
Oakland, CA 94607
tel: (510) 893 8555   TOLL FREE: 800 275-8555
fax: (510) 893 8563
e-mail: info@lonelyplanet.com

FRANCE
71 bis rue du Cardinal Lemoine, 75005 Paris
tel: 1 44 32 06 20   fax: 1 46 34 72 55
e-mail: 100560.415@compuserve.com

World Wide Web: http://www.lonelyplanet.com/

KENYA TRAVEL ATLAS

Dear Traveller,

We would appreciate it if you would take the time to write your thoughts on this page and return it to a Lonely Planet office. Only with your help can we continue to make sure this atlas is as accurate and travel-friendly as possible.

Where did you acquire this atlas?

Bookstore ☐   In which section of the store did you find it, i.e. maps or travel guidebooks? ....

Map shop ☐   Direct mail ☐   Other ....

How are you using this travel atlas?

On the road ☐   For home reference ☐   For business reference ☐

Other ....

When travelling with this atlas, did you find any inaccuracies?

....

....

....

How does the atlas fare on the road in terms of ease of use and durability?

....

Are you using the atlas in conjunction with an LP guidebook/s?   Yes ☐   No ☐

Which one/s?...

Have you bought any other LP products for your trip?..

Do you think the information on the travel atlas maps is presented clearly?   Yes ☐   No ☐

If English is not your main language, do you find the language sections useful?   Yes ☐   No ☐

Please list any features you think should be added to the travel atlas.

....

....

....

Would you consider purchasing another atlas in this series?   Yes ☐   No ☐

Please indicate your age group.

15-25 ☐   26-35 ☐   36-45 ☐   46-55 ☐   56-65 ☐   66+ ☐

Do you have any other general comments you'd like to make?

....

....

....

....

....

P.S. Thank you very much for this information. The best contributions will be rewarded with a free copy of a Lonely Planet book. We give away lots of books, but, unfortunately, not every contributor receives one.

Notes